Bernhard Pick

The Talmud

What it is and What it Knows about Jesus and his Followers

Bernhard Pick

The Talmud
What it is and What it Knows about Jesus and his Followers

ISBN/EAN: 9783744648448

Printed in Europe, USA, Canada, Australia, Japan

Cover: Foto ©Lupo / pixelio.de

More available books at **www.hansebooks.com**

THE

TALMUD

WHAT IT IS

AND WHAT IT KNOWS ABOUT JESUS AND HIS FOLLOWERS.

BY
REV. BERNHARD PICK, Ph.D.

———

NEW YORK:
JOHN B. ALDEN, PUBLISHER.
1887.

DEDICATED

TO THE

REV. PHILIP SCHAFF, D.D., LL.D.

PROFESSOR IN THE UNION THEOLOGICAL
SEMINARY, NEW YORK.

PREFACE.

It is a saying of Monsieur Rénan that "in the history of the origins of Christianity, the Talmud has hitherto been far too much neglected." His idea is that the New Testament can only be understood by the light of the Talmud, while the present work will prove that many things in the Talmud can only be understood by the light of the New Testament and the history of the Church. To do this we have divided the matter into two parts. The first tries to show *what the Talmud is*, by giving a succinct history of the development of Jewish traditionalism, which culminated in the Talmud, "that wonderful monument of human industry, human wisdom, and human folly," as Milman calls it ; and in order to dispel erroneous views concerning the Talmud, we have arrayed the opinions of such scholars as Milman, Farrar, Geikie, Schaff, Delitzsch and others, whom no one will accuse of partiality. As a connecting link we have inserted those passages of the Talmud which treat of the Messiah, because we believe that their contents were more or less influenced by Christian thought, and that they do not express the views of the Jews concerning the Messiah before and at the Christian era. For, says Mr. Stanton (*The Jewish and the Christian Messiah*, Edinburgh, 1886): "Is it possible, then, that we should put implicit confidence even in the Talmud—the oldest portion of which is allowed not to have been

v

brought to its final form before the close of
the second century—not to say in later Rabbinic writings, for a true representation of
the Messianic doctrine before and at the
Christian era?"

The second part brings before the reader
what the Talmud has to say about Jesus,
the gospels and Christian customs, which
can only be understood by the light of the
New Testament. In order to be as complete as possible, we have inserted all those
passages which are now no more found in
the Talmud, but which are conveniently
given in a little pamphlet published by
Meklenburg at Königsberg, entitled *Kwotz-*
oth ha-hashmatoth, and which may also be
seen scattered in Levy's *Neuhebräisches Lex-*
icon. All these passages speak for themselves, and their value is enhanced by the
very fact that they are extant in a work
which from its very nature was compiled by
persons antagonistic to Christianity. Thus,
for instance, what is narrated about James,
at least shows the importance of his position
in the traditional recollections of the Jews,
and it is very interesting to know that even
before the destruction of Jerusalem, the
Christian Sunday had already become so
prominent among the first Christians, that
the Jews would not even fast on that day—
which would necessitate a rest from labor—
in order not to be identified with the Naza-
renes. The Talmud also corroborates the
fact that certain sayings of Jesus, now no
more extant in the gospels, were current
among his disciples. Many are found in the
writings of the Apostolic Fathers, as may be
seen from the notes to the "Sayings of
Christ," as published in our *Apocryphal Life*
of Jesus, p. 124 *seq.;* 184 *seq.;* two are here
quoted from the Talmud, and how many

more may be contained in this voluminous work, couched in words now no more intelligent or as cryptographs. Thus, *e. g.*, Saul, the disciple of Gamaliel, a Pharisee of the Pharisees, and who before and after his conversion was such a prominent personage at Jerusalem, is nowhere mentioned in the Talmud, although his teacher is so often named. And yet while his name is not mentioned, it is claimed by a modern Jewish writer that in a passage of the Talmud, where Gamaliel and a certain disciple argue with one another, that this certain disciple is none else than the Apostle Paul. As the Christian will undoubtedly be interested in this matter, we reproduce here the following, from our article " The Apostle Paul in the Talmud," as published in the New York *Independent*, (May 5, 1887). The passage as found in *Shabbath*, fol. 30, col. 2, runs thus :—

Rabban Gamaliel was sitting one day expounding to his disciples, that in the Messianic age it would come to pass that the curse pronounced in Paradise on woman would be removed, and that a woman would be able to bear a child every day, for it is said: She travails and brings forth at once (*Jer.* xxxi. 8). " *That disciple*," laughing at this, said: " Rabbi, it is written, ' There is nothing new under the sun '" (*Eccl.* i. 9). Said Gamaliel to him : " Come, and I will show you instances even in this dispensation." He went out and showed him hens (which lay eggs every day). Another day Rabban Gamaliel was sitting and explaining that in future the trees would bear fruit every day, for it is said: " And it shall bring forth boughs and bear fruit " (*Ezek.* xvii. 23), as a tree shall produce boughs every day, so it shall likewise bear fruit. " *That disciple* " laughing at this, said: " Rabbi, it is written, ' There is no new thing under the sun.' " Said Gamaliel, " Come, and I will show instances in this world." He went out and pointed to the caperberry. Again Gamaliel was sitting and expounding that in future the land of Israel would produce cakes and clothes of the finest wool, for it is said · " There shall be an abundance of corn in the earth " (*Ps.* lxxii. 16). " *That disciple*," laughing again, said : " There is no new thing under the sun." Gamaliel said : " Come, and I will show thee instances in this world." He went out, and showed him cakes and mushrooms, and the fine bark which surrounds the soft twigs of the date palm. From this passage Dr. Bloch (*Studien zur Geschichte der Sammlung der althebräischen Literatur*, Leipsic, 1875, p. 155) argues as follows : Gamaliel was controverting the idea that the Messianic prophesies were accomplished in the person of Jesus, since a redeemer could not have atoned for the sins of the world, and have left in full force the penalty pronounced in Paradise. Not only the guilt of sin, but the effects of sin were, according to him, to be done away in the Messianic age. The pupil presses his master by telling that all such ideas were contrary to the words, "There is nothing new under the sun." Gamaliel rejoins that there is no opposition between his views and the text quoted by his pupil, inasmuch as even a superficial examination of Nature showed that the fulfilment of his expectations would require nothing absolutely new. The person of that pupil, Bloch continues, is none else than the Apostle Paul, for the following reasons: 1. That disciple must have been a well-known individual, who had achieved a certain fame and popularity. The expression אורו תלמור points to this, and reminds very much of אותי חאיש which is used in the Talmud for the founder of Christianity. 2. That he was no stranger to the Pharisees, but one who belonged to their school, although opposed to many of their views and disposed to ridicule the same, as the word לגלג shows. He was one who was not loved by them, as is shown by the intentional suppression of his name. "Recollections of a painful character," says Bloch, "were connected with the name [of the anonymous disciple] which the Talmud, according to its usual custom, did not wish to reserve." 3. He was a pupil of Gamaliel. 4. Gamaliel's answer contained a vigorous attack upon Christianity. "That disciple" opposes him and tries to convince him, and shows a zeal in the matter which proves that the point in question was of great importance to him. With a conspicuous constancy he opposes his teacher again and again, and has no regard for the position of the pupil toward his master. Yea, it even appears that he tried to show by all means that Gamaliel's theory concerning the Messiah was in opposition with Scripture. "In a word," says this Jewish writer, "we have brought before us in the narrative of the Talmud, a very well-known disputant on the side of Christianity and pupil of Gamaliel, well acquainted with the Rabbinical mode of argumentation—therefore, no other than the fiery and zealous Apostle Paul." If indeed it could be proven that this Gamaliel is really the teacher of Paul, and not Gamaliel II.—and as it stands in the Talmud there is nothing to militate against it—the above controversy would be an important contribution to the life of the great Apostle.

Should this volume prove acceptable, it is intended to publish an English translation of the first treatise of the Talmud, entitled *Berachoth*, which is already in manuscript.

By the publication of *Berachoth*—which will
be the first English translation ever published—the reader will have a full idea of the
Talmud in every respect.

B. PICK.

ALLEGHENY, Pa., *August*, 1887.

THE TALMUD.

PART I.

JEWISH tradition reached its climax in the Talmud, "that wonderful monument," as Milman calls it, "of human industry, human wisdom, and human folly." "The Talmud," says a modern writer—

" May compete with the *Constitutions* of Loyola for the right to be considered the most irresistible organ ever forged for the subjugation of the human will. It stands quite alone, its age and origin considered, as a means of perpetuating a definite system of religious bondage. By the *Constitutions*, while the education of the young is committed as far as possible to the subtle manipulation of the Order of Jesus, the decisive appeal to the obedience of the neophyte is made, once and for all, at a fixed opportunity. When made as directed by the founder, it is said never to have been known to fail. But the Talmud not only awaits the infant at birth and regulates every incident of that event (even to the names of angels that are to be inscribed on the door, and the words on the four corners of the apartment), but anticipates each circumstance from the earliest moment of probability. In every relation of life, in every action, in every conceivable circumstance—for food, dress, habit, language, devotion, relaxation—it prescribes almost every word to be uttered, and almost every thought to be conceived. Its rule is minute, omnipresent, inflexible. Its severity is never relaxed. To borrow an illustration from the founder: the Jewish mind, subjected while in a fusible state to this iron mould, has been at once chilled and case-hardened by its pressure." [1].

The Talmud as we now have it, is not the work of one, but of many generations, and its origin may be traced back to the resto-

---

1. *Edinburgh Review*, July, 1873. p. 18.

ration of the Jewish commonwealth under
Ezra, the historic originator of the oral law.
"He carried on," says Farrar, "the silent
revolution in Jewish conceptions of which
the last eight chapters of the book of Ezekiel
are the indication, and which find expression
also in the book of Chronicles. In Ezekiel
we see the gradual passing of the prophet
into the scribe, in whom prophecy finds it
necessary to take the form of law, and who
for glowing ideal visions furnishes a legisla-
tive code."[1]

After the return from the Babylonish captivity, Ezra attempted to restore the Jewish
polity to its former state, but he found his
countrymen, although on the whole relig-
iously inclined, yet much neglected, and
consequently very ignorant. In order to
bring about the necessary reformation, Ezra
is said to have associated with himself some
of the most eminent men of the age, as an
organized college or synod, commonly called
the *Great Synagogue*, which terminated with
the life of Simon the Just, its last surviving
member. By the zealous efforts of these
enlightened men the institutes were happily
re-established, or to use the language of Talmud, [2] "As soon as the men of the Great
Synagogue met together, they restored the
law to its pristine glory," and an efficient and
extensive provision was made for the spiritual and moral culture of the people. Under
their influence arose a distinct order of men,
who devoted themselves to the work of public instruction. Bearing the name of *Soferim* or Scribes, γϛαμματεἲϛ, they became the
teaching clergy of the Jews, the authorized
expositors of the Holy Scriptures, and ed-

1. *History of Interpretation* (New York, 1886). p. 52.
2 *Jerus Megilla*, *III. in fine.*

itors of the sacred text. The influence
which they thus gained, the fact that from
the paucity of books and the general ignorance, the people depended *entirely* on this
religious aristocracy, together with the growing tendencies of the age in that direction,
contributed not a little to place religious
eminence in mere knowledge and outward
observances, without spiritual experience of
love. " Piety dwindled into legalism. Salvation was identified with outward con-
formity. A torturing scrupulosity was substituted for a glad obedience. God's righteous faithfulness was treated as a forensic
covenant. For prophecy there was only the
miserable substitute of the 'Daughter of a
Voice'; for faith the sense of merit acquired by legal exactitude. The 'pious'
were hopelessly identified with the party
of the Scribes. The Synagogues became
schools. Ethics were subordinated to Lit-
urgiology. Messianism was debased into an
unmeaning phrase or a materialized fable.
The pride of pedantry, despising moral
nobleness, and revelling in an hypocrisy so
profound as hardly to recognize that it was
hypocritical, wrapped itself in an esoteric
theology, and looked down on the children
of a common Father as an accursed multitude in whose very touch there was ceremonial defilement. This was the ultimate
result of that recrudescense of ceremonial
which was the special work of the scholars
of Ezra. And of this work the basis was a
perverted Bibliolatry, and the instrument an
elaborate exegesis."[1] The position of the
Scribes also laid the foundation of the exag-
gerated notions which both teachers and
taught afterwards formed of the dignity of

---

[1]. Farrar, *l c.*, p. 58 *seq.*

the rabbi or teacher, and we must therefore not be surprised when we read: "To be against the word of the scribes is more punishable than to be against the word of the Bible;"[1] "The voice of the rabbi is as the voice of God,"[2] and "He who transgresses the word of the scribes throws away his life."[3]

The men of the great synagogue left one maxim behind them: "Be deliberate in judgment, make many disciples, and make a hedge about the law."[4] "The hedge," says Farrar, "was made; its construction was regarded as the main function of Rabbinism;

---

1. *Sanhedrin* xi. 3.   2. *Erubin*, fol. 21, col. 2.
3. *Berachoth*, fol. 4, col. 2.
4. *Aboth*, I., 1. The late Dean Stanley, in quoting this sentence says: "But there is one traditional saying ascribed to the Great Synagogue which must surely have come from an early stage in the history of the scribes, and which well illustrates the disease, to which as to a parasitical plant, the order itself and all the branches into which it has grown, has been subject. It resembles in form the famous mediæval motto for the guidance of conventual ambition, although it is more serious in spirit: 'Be deliberate,' etc. Nothing could be less like the impetuosity, the simplicity, or the openness of Ezra than any of these three precepts. But the one which in each succeeding generation predominated more and more was the last: 'Make a hedge about the law.' To build up elaborate explanations, thorny obstructions, subtle evasions, enormous developments, was the labor of the late Jewish scribes, till the Pentateuch was buried beneath the Mishna, and the Mishna beneath the Gemara. To make hedges round the koran has been, though not perhaps in equally disproportioned manner, the aim of the schools of El-Azar and Cordova, and of the successive Fetvaks of the Sheykhs-et-Islam. To erect hedges round the gospel has been the effort, happily not continuous or uniform, but of large and dominant sections of the tribes of Christianity, and the words of its founder have well-nigh disappeared behind the successive intrenchments, and fences, and outposts, and counterworks of councils, and synods, and popes, and anti-popes, and sums of theology and of saving doctrine, of confessions of faith and schemes of salvation, and the world has again and again sighed for one who would once more speak with the authority of self-evidencing truth, and 'not as the scribes,' (Matthew vii. 29). A distinguished Jewish rabbi of this century, in a striking and pathetic passage on this crisis in the history of his nation, contrasts the prospect of the course which Ezekiel and Isaiah had indicated with that which was adopted by Ezra, and sums up his reflections with the remark that 'Had the spirit been preserved instead of the letter, the substance instead of the form, then Judaism might have been spared the necessity of Christianity' (Herzfeld ii. 32-36). But we in like manner say that had the scribes of the Christian church retained more of the genius of the Hebrew prophets, Christianity in its turn would have been spared what has too often been a return to Judaism, and it was in the perception of the superiority of the prophet to the scribe that its original force and unique excellence have consisted.'" (*Lect. on the History of the Jewish Church*, vol. III., p. 165, *seq.* New York, 1877.)

it excluded all light from without and all
egress from within ; but it was so carefully
cultivated that the shrine itself was totally
disregarded. The oral law was first exalted
as a necessary supplement to the written law ;
then substituted in the place of it, and finally
identified with the inferences of the Rabbis." .
(*l. c.*, p. 62.)

The last surviving member of the Great
Synagogue was, according to tradition,
Simon I., the Just, whose recorded maxim
was : " The world stands on three things—the
law, temple-service and well-doing." [1] With
Simon ended that class of teachers who were
styled *Soferim* or scribes, and who were followed by the *Tanaïm* or teachers of the
law, the νομοδιδάσκαλοι of the New Testament.
The Tanaïm continued the work of their
predecessors, the Soferim, by expounding
more definitely their views and expanding
the same, and the laws thus laid down, called
Halachoth, constitute the contents of the
present Mishna, and the oldest commentaries
on the Pentateuch, such as the *Mechilta* on
Exodus, *Sifra* on Leviticus, and *Sifre* on
Numbers and Deuteronomy.

The first of these Tanaïm was Antigonus of
Socho (about 200–170 B.C.). He was a disciple of Simon the Just, and the first who
bears a Greek name. His recorded maxim :
" Be not like servants who serve their master
for the sake of reward, but be like servants
who serve their master without looking for·a
reward, and let the fear of Heaven be upon
you," [2] is, according to Stanley, " full of significance and shows how a seed of future
faith had already borne fruit in that dark and
troubled time." Another writer calls this
precept " a noble and almost evangelical one.

---

1. *Aboth*, I., 2.　　　　2. *Ibid.* I., 3.

Truly a most beautiful maxim and one de-
noting a legitimate reaction from the legal
formalism which was in process of development."[1]   According to Jewish tradition the
maxim of Antigonus is claimed to have been
the origin of Sadduceeism, a view now generally rejected by modern critics.

The next teachers were José ben Joëser
and José ben Jochanan (about 150 B.C.).
That they were not the direct successors of
Antigonus, we infer from the reading : "They
received the tradition from *them*," and not
from "*him*."   Little is known of their peculiar
teaching.   Their fundamental principles are
somewhat vague, but point in the direction
of increasing rabbinical influence and preten-
sion. The first, who was of Zereda said : " Let
thy house be a meeting place for the wise ;
dust thyself with the dust of their feet, and
eagerly drink in their words."[2]   The second,
who was of Jerusalem, said : " Let thy house
be wide open, and let the poor be the children of thy house.   Do not multiply speech
with a woman.   If this applies to one's own
wife, how much more to that of another
man ?   Hence the sages say, that the man
who multiplies speech with a woman bring-
eth evil upon himself, swerves from the
word of the law, and will finally inherit destruction."[3]   Both these teachers were held
in great esteem, and, at their decease it was
said : " Those in whom every excellency was
found had now departed."[4]

To them succeeded Joshua ben Perachia
and Nithai of Arbela.   The recorded maxim
of the former is : " Procure for thyself a
teacher, gain to thyself a friend, and judge

---

[1]. Pressensé, *Jesus Christ, His Life, Times and Work*, New York, 1868, p. 68, *seq.*
[2]. *Aboth*, I., 4, 5.   [3]. *Aboth*, I., 4, 5.   [4]. *Sotah*, fol. 47, col. 1.

all men charitably;"[1] that of the latter is: "Keep aloof from a wicked neighbor, have no fellowship with sinners, and reject not the belief in retribution."[2] By a strange anachronism some Jewish writers declare that Joshua was the teacher of Jesus.

As next teachers we mention Judah ben Tabbaï and Simon ben Shetach (about 90–70 B.C.). The latter was a brother-in-law of King Alexander Jannaeus, and when at one time a persecution ensued against the then dominating spiritual leaders of the people, Simon escaped to Egypt, where he joined his former teacher, Joshua. Through the influence of his sister, the queen, Simon was soon recalled, and having received pardon for his friend and teacher, Simon communicated the intelligence to Joshua, who soon returned. Tabbaï's maxim was: "Be not like the orderers of judges. When parties are before thee, regard them as transgressors of the law, but regard them as innocent immediately after they are released, and have suffered the penalty of the law."[3] That of Simon was: "Be extremely careful in examining witnesses, and beware lest from thy mode of questioning they should learn how to give false testimony."[4] He was the first who inaugurated a complete system of education throughout the country. Under his influence, for the first time, schools were established in every large provincial town, and all boys from six years and upwards were compelled to attend them.

The next famous teachers were Shemaiah and Abtalion. The recorded maxim of the first is : "Love a trade, hate lordship, and do not obtrude thyself upon the powers that

---

1. *Aboth.* I., 6.   3. *Ibid.* I., 8.
2. *Ibid.* I., 7.   4. *Ibid.* I., 9.

2

be," [1] whilst the latter said : " Ye sages, be on
your guard with respect to your words, lest
ye become amenable to captivity, and be exiled to a place of evil waters, and the disciples
who come after you may drink of the same
and die, whereby the name of God would be
blasphemed." [2]   On the death of these two
teachers there were no qualified successors to
take their place, and two sons of Bethera,
otherwise unknown, occupied it for a time.
They were discussing one of the trivial
ceremonial questions which then, as on later
occasions, both in the Jewish and Christian
church, preoccupied the main interest of
theological schools.   It was the grave prob-
lem (as it seemed to them) whether the
Paschal lamb might be killed on the Sabbath.
In their perplexity, they asked : " Was there
none present who had been a disciple of the
two who had been so honored ? " (*viz.:*
Shemaiah and Abtalion.)   The question was
answered by Hillel, the Babylonian.   He
solved the difficulty with reasons from analogy, from the text and from the context.
They refused his decision, until he ended by
saying : " Thus have I heard from my masters, Shemaiah and Abtalion."   This was
decisive.   Having before been regarded as
a stranger from Babylon, he was now welcomed as chief.   " Whose fault was it,". he
said, " that you had recourse to a Babylonian ?   You have not paid due attention to
Shemaiah and Abtalion, the two great men
of the age, who were with you all the time."
His presidency in the Sanhedrin is given,
according to treatise, *Shabbath,* fol. 15, col. 1,
as about one hundred years before the destruction of Jerusalem.

---

1. *Aboth.* I., 10.   2. *Ibid.* I., 11.

HILLEL I., THE GREAT, OR THE ELDER.

FOR more than one reason Hillel deserves to be noticed a little more fully than his predecessors, although it is difficult to separate history from legend [1] and truth from fiction in the many stories which the Talmud relates of him. " It has been reserved," says Stanley, " for modern times to recognize his extraordinary merit," but we may also say " to exaggerate his merit," as was done especially by Rénan [2] and Geiger, [3] against whom Professor Delitzsch of Leipsic published his famous treatise, *Jesus and Hillel compared with Reference to Rénan and Geiger,* [4] from which the following extracts are given : " About fifty years before our present era the following occurred at Jerusalem. [5] Shemaiah and Abtalion, the most celebrated teachers of that age, spent on a certain occasion the whole of the night from Friday to Saturday in directing the studies of a large number of disciples. It was in the month of Tebeth, about the time of the winter solstice —hence toward the close of December. When the auroral column had arisen—so

1. Thus for instance we read that " Hillel knew all languages, even the language of mountains, hills and valleys, trees, vegetables, wild and tame beasts, and demons " (Soferim, XVI., 9), or that he " had eighty disciples ; thirty of them were worthy that the Shechina should rest upon them as upon Moses ; thirty, that the sun should stand still at their command as at that of Joshua ; and twenty were only moderately learned ; but the greatest of all was Jonathan ben Uziel of whom it is said, that when he studied the law, every bird that flew over his head was at once burned up." (Succa, fol. 28, col. 1)

2 In his *Vie de Jesus,* he said : " Hillel was the real teacher of Jesus, if we may say teacher when speaking of so lofty an originality (*Hillel fut le vrai maitre de Jesus, s'il est permis de parler de maitre quand ils'agit d'une si haute originalité, p. 35.*)

3. In his lectures on " Judaism and History (1864), Dr. Abr. Geiger (d. 1874), the champion of Jewish reform says, " Jesus was a Pharisee who walked in the paths of Hillel. He never gave utterance to a new idea (*Einen neuen Gedanken sprach er keineswegs aus.*)

4 Translated into English by the Rev. B. Pick (*Andover Review,* September and November, 1884).

5. *Yoma,* fol. 35, col. 2.

the Shemitic would put it, because the sun suddenly rising there, appears above the horizon like a cone of light—Shemaiah said to Abtalion: 'Dear brother Abtalion, it is usually light in our school by day; it must be cloudy this morning to be so dark!' As they looked up, however, they discovered that there was something in the shape of a human being before the window. They climbed up, and found a man actually buried in the snow, which had fallen during the night. It was *Hillel*. They took him out of the snow, put him into a bath, rubbed him with oil, and brought him near to a fire, for they said: 'He is worthy, that for his sake we should break the Sabbath.'"

But how came Hillel to be found thus placed before the window? This Hillel, the grandfather of that Gamaliel, at whose feet sat the apostle Paul, the ancestor of a family within which for centuries the presidency of the Sanhedrin was transmitted, was the son of a poor exiled family in Babylon. The family was reduced, although it could trace its pedigree back to King David. [1]

Hillel, as well as his brother Shebna [2] had gone to Jerusalem—the one to try his fortune in business, the other to satisfy his thirst for knowledge at the great seat of national learning. In order to carry this into effect, he engaged himself as a day-laborer, and earned a *tropaïcon* daily. This was the Greek name for the Roman *victoriatus,* a small coin worth half a denarius, upon which the image of Victoria, the Goddess of Victory, had been

---

1. *Bereshith Rabba*, section 98.
2. *Sota*, fol, 21, col. 1, according to which, after it was too late and in order to please God, he offered to divide the gain with his brother.

stamped. One-half of his daily earnings had to suffice for the maintenance of his family (for he was married); the other half be paid as fee for admission to the *beth-ha-midrash*, the institution over which Shemaiah and Abtalion presided. One day, however, he failed in obtaining labor, and was not allowed to enter the college. Favored by the darkness of the night he climbed up to the window late on Friday evening, and placed himself so that he could see and hear everything. But unable long to brave the cold and ceaseless December snow, which sometimes falls in Jerusalem, he fell into that state of numbness from which he was with difficulty resuscitated the following Sabbath morning.

Thus *Hillel* became what he was. He sought to satisfy his thirst for knowledge among the most renowned masters of his time, and spared no trouble in becoming the heir of their knowledge. Having attended the lectures of the highest authorities regarding questions of the law, he soon became one of those highest authorities regarding questions of the law. When at one time the question was debated, whether it was lawful to kill the paschal lamb on the day of preparation for the feast, when that day is the Sabbath, Hillel declared that it is lawful, in accordance with genuine tradition.[1] From that time on he was looked upon as one of the most prominent teachers of the so-called oral or traditional law. He secured respect for the law by his great learning, his personal good qualities, and his moderation, and that at a time of general national decay and irreligion. But he never became a reformer. Dr. Geiger is the first to give him this name, and he does it merely as an attempt to disparage Jesus. Re-

---

1. *Pesachim*, fol. 68, col. 1 ; *Jerus. Pesachim*, fol. 33, col.1.

former, in the good sense of the word, is one
who is endued with creative energy, one who
brings back the religion of a nation which had
become defaced and deformed to its original
state, and thus breathes new life into a great
community, like that which it originally pos-
sessed.   Samuel and Ezra were reformers
of this class. Hillel changed nothing. He
left things as he found them. It is indeed
true that he introduced a few innovations
in the civil laws, especially concerning lending
money and buying and selling, which suggest
cunning contrivances for evading the laws of
Moses ; but in other respects all he did was
to carry out more fully the system of tradition taught by the Pharisees ; he gave himself no trouble as to the religious state of
the nation at large, and did nothing whatever to awaken religious life, which was in
such a decayed state, or to give it a new
impulse.   Hillel's activity was not in the
least reformatory, much less creative. It
consisted essentially in nothing else than in
the development of the so-called oral law,
which aimed to ascertain the intent of the
Mosaic statutes, in accordance with certain
rules of interpretation, and to protect them
against infringement by a hedge of new traditions. In this legal overstraining of the
Mosaic law, Hillel had an equal rival in the
more strict and, regarding ceremonial things,
more painstaking Shammai.

An example will show in how far at that
time the spirit of the law of Moses was already given up. In Exodus xvi. 5, we have
the indirect commandment that everything
necessary for the Sabbath should be prepared on the sixth day. The meaning and
object is clear: Rest on the Sabbath, which
according to the law of Moses should be observed by the man-servant and maid-servant,

as well as by the master and mistress,
should not be disturbed by kitchen work.
The scribes, however, raised the question,
whether an egg which a hen had laid on a
Sabbath could be eaten on that day. One
should suppose that common sense would
have settled this question, inasmuch as in
the laying of eggs, man takes no active part ;
but it was decided that the eating of such an
egg was unconditionally prohibited, in case
it was laid by a hen designed for this purpose, since in that case it was the result of
work [begun on a week-day and] brought to
an end on the Sabbath, hence unlawful.
On this the "fathers of antiquity"[1] were
unanimous. But how would it be if the hen
were one intended not to lay eggs, but for
eating, and how, if a Sabbath and a feast-
day, observed as a Sabbath, should come together? On this point, Shammai, against
his custom, was less strict than Hillel, and
decided that it was lawful to eat the egg of
a hen, itself destined to be eaten, on which-
ever day the egg had been laid. Hillel,
however, the "Reformer," according to Geiger, the "real teacher of Jesus," according
to Rénan, argued as follows :—Since the
egg has come to maturity on a Sabbath or
feast-day, and is therefore of unlawful origin,
it is not allowed to make use of it on such a
day; and although it would be lawful to
make use of the egg of such a hen, laid on a
feast-day or Sabbath not followed or preced-
ed by another similarly sacred day, yet it
must not be eaten if two such days come together, because, otherwise, there would be a
temptation to use it on the second holy day.
And since it is forbidden even to carry un-

---

1. Thus (אבות הָעֵולְם) Hillel and Shammai are called in the Mishna *Eduyoth* 1, 4.

lawful food from one place to another, such
an egg must not only not be eaten, but must
not be picked up nor put aside; whereby it
is self-evident that the conscientious man is
not to put a finger on it, for *that* might lead
to his taking it altogether into his hand, and
is not even to look at it, for *that* might pos-
sibly make him wish he could eat it.   In this
famous dispute about the egg,[1] as in similar
ones, Hillel was right against Shammai, for
a voice from heaven (bath kol) is said to
have been heard, saying: "The words of
both are the words of the living God, but the
rule of the school of Hillel is to be followed."[2]

Of the many stories concerning Hillel,
Delitzsch gives the following:

Two men—we are told in the Talmud—quarrelled with
each other in Jerusalem. "Now and never!" said the
one, "400 *sus* (a coin worth a Roman denarius, bearing
the image of Zeus) to the man, who should put Hillel out
of temper." "Done!" exclaimed the other. It was a
Friday afternoon, and Hillel was washing and combing his
hair for the Sabbath. At this unseasonable time, and
without addressing him by his becoming title, some one
before his door shouted: "Is Hillel here?" He (Hillel)
wrapped his mantle round him, came out and said: "My
son, what is your desire?"   "I have a question to ask,"
replied the coarse fellow. "Ask on, my son," said Hillel.
"Why have the Babylonians such unsightly round
heads?" asked the man. He (Hillel) said: "A very important question didst thou ask, my son," [the reason is]
"because their midwives are not clever." He (the man)
went away, and after having waited an hour he returned
and said: "Where is Hillel? where is Hillel?" He
(Hillel) threw on his mantle and went out and said to him:
"My son, what hast thou?" He replied: "I want to ask a
question." "Ask on, my son," he said. "Why have the
Thermudians such narrow eyelids?" "An important question, my son," said Hillel. "Because they live in a sandy
country." Again the man went away, and in another

---

1. A whole Talmudical treatise, which treats of the festival days
in general, is entitled *Beza* (the egg) from the first word with which
it commences.
2. *Eruhin*, fol. 13, col. 2. That Hillel's rule was preferred, was
because his disciples were gentle and forbearing, referred to the
decisions maintained by the school of Shammai and even mentioned them first.

hour's time he returned as before saying: "Where is Hillel? where is Hillel?" He threw on his mantle and went out and said to him: "My son, what hast thou?" He replied: "I wish to ask a question." "Ask on, my son," he said. "Why have the Africans such broad feet?" "Indeed, a very important question, my son," said Hillel. "Because they live in a marshy land." He (the man) said to him: "I have many more questions to ask, but I am afraid lest I only try thy patience and make thee angry." Hillel, drawing his mantle around him, sat down and bade the man to ask all the questions he wished. "So" said the man, thoroughly disarmed: "art thou Hillel whom they call a prince in Israel?" He replied, "Yes." "Well," said the man, "I pray there may not be many more in Israel like thee." "And why, my son?" said Hillel. "Because," said the man, "I have lost four hundred *sus* on thy account." "Calm thyself, my son," replied Hillel; "better that thou shouldst lose four hundred *sus*, and four hundred more for Hillel's sake, than that Hillel should lose his temper."[1]

So great was Hillel's good nature. It was boundless. For a rich man who had been impoverished, he hired a saddle-horse and halberdier, and as he could obtain none, he is said to have once taken his place for three miles.[2] Indeed his good nature transcended the bounds of truth, for while Shammai demanded the truth in the bridal song concerning the appearance of the bride, Hillel taught that, however ugly she were, one must put himself in the place of the bridegroom and sing: "Ah the lovely and charming bride!"[3] Yes, in his beneficence for the sake of peace, Hillel showed a want of veracity; for once, by means of a cunning trick, he passed an ox for a cow, which he offered as a sacrifice in the temple-court, in order to avoid a dispute with the followers of Shammai concerning a question of the law.[4] Only because his

---

1. *Shabbath*, fol. 30, col. 2; fol. 31, col. 1.
2. *Kethuboth*, fol. 67, col. 2.
3. Ibid. fol. 16, col. 2; fol. 17, col. 1.
4. He wagged the tail of the animal, to hide its sex. The story is given in Tr. *Beza*, fol. 20, col. 1. Jost (*Geschichte des Judenthums* I, 267) says: "Hillel did not only suffer himself to be intimidated by Shammai, but even yielded to his boldest disciples in such a manner in the Temple-court, that he told an untruth in order to avoid a dispute, a circumstance which the rabbis attributed to him as a great merit."

famous meekness had its dark, as well as its
bright sides, we can understand how he, under the absolute monarchy of the first Herod,
who showed cowardice towards Rome, and
cruelty toward his own people, could maintain the highest national honorary position
in Jerusalem in an unmolested and even
favored manner, and that he attained, according to tradition, [1] like Moses, the age
of one hundred and twenty years. Another
story of Hillel runs thus: Once a Gentile
came to Shammai, and said: "Make me a
proselyte; but you must teach me the whole
law during the time that I can stand on one
leg." Shammai got angry and drove him
away with a stick which he held in his hand.
He went to Hillel with the same challenge.
Hillel converted him by answering him on
the spot: "That which is hateful to thyself,
do not do to thy neighbor. This is the
whole law, and the rest is mere commentary." [2]   This is the famous answer, which
modern Jewish writers quote with a show
of self-complacency, and upon which rest
Rénan's and Geiger's assertions concerning
Jesus.

Passing over the different apophthegms of
Hillel, which are scattered in the *Pirke
Aboth* and other parts of the Mishna, we
must mention that he was the first who reduced the Chaotic mass of rules which had
gathered round the Mosaic precepts to Six
Orders—the first oral basis of the future
Mishna, and also drew up the seven exegetic
rules which were the basis of all later developments of the Oral Law.   From the captivity the Jews brought with them a reveren-
tial, or, rather, a passionate, attachment to

---

1. *Bereshith Rabba*, section 100.
2. *Shabbath*, fol. 31, col. 1. Of this sentence we shall speak further
on.

the Mosaic law. By degrees, attachment to the law sunk deeper and deeper into the national character: it was not merely at once their Bible and their statute-book; it entered into the most minute detail of common life. But no written law can provide for all possible exigencies. In order to adapt it to all possible or impossible cases, the Law became a deep and intricate study and developed itself into that homiletico-exegetical literature which was called *Midrash*, *i.e.*, exposition. The midrash was at first simple, but in the course of time it again developed itself into the *Halakha*,[1] *i.e.*, "decision," norm, systematized legal precept, and *Haggada*,[2] *i.e.*, "what was said," without having the authority of the law, *i.e.*, *free exposition*, *homilies*, *moral sayings*, and *legends*. Starting from the principle that Scripture, especially the Pentateuch, contained an answer to every question, the text was explained in a fourfold manner, viz. 1, *Peshat* in a simple, primary, or literal ; 2, *Derush*, or secondary, homiletic, or spiritual ; 3, *Remez*, *i.e.*, allegori-

---

1. A writer in the *Cornhill Magazine* (August, 1875) says : "The Talmudic Dictionary reminds us of Tennyson's description of the Sangraal, when it defines Halaca as a "thing which goes and comes from the beginning to the end." The words of the wise which were likened by the preacher to "goads and nails fixed by masters of assemblies," are probably these Halacas. They contain specimens of Hebrew dialectic, which as little as the words of some Jews of later time bear out the assertion of Adam Clarke, conceived in these carefully distinguished and philosophic terms : "The Jews ever have been the most puerile, absurd, and ridiculous reasoners in the world, always excepting of course," adds the reverend writer by a lucky afterthought, "the inspired writers."

2. "Heine," says the same writer in the *Cornhill Magazine*, in his *Romancero*, following the unerring instinct of the poet, "has given some remarkable information about the Talmud. He is pleased to call the Agada a garden, and the Halaca a fighting school. It is probably true, as Deutsch observed, that he had never read a word of either. The Agada is a strange *pot pourri* of legend, rhetoric and philosophy. It infuses, says one who knew it well, doubt and solicitude into the mind by its secret sense." Mr. Deutsch (art. *Talmud*) says, "If the Halakha was the iron bulwark around the nationality of Israel, the Haggada was a maze of flowery walks within those fortress walls," an ! "between the rugged boulders of the Law there grow the blue flowers of romance and poetry—parable, gnome, tale, saga—its elements are taken from heaven and earth ; but chiefly and most lovingly from Scripture and from the human heart."

cal; 4, Sôd, *i.e.*, recondite, or mysterious sense, which was afterwards designated by the acrostic PaRDeS. The fourfold mode, however, was not sufficient for the explanation, and, according to the old saying that "the law can be interpreted in forty-nine different modes" (*Midrash Rabb. Levit.* section xxvi. p. 149*b*), all impossibilities could be made possible. Hence the necessity arose for laying down and fixing certain laws for the interpretation of the Scripture. This was done by Hillel by his seven rules, according to which the law was to be explained, viz.:—1, inference from minor to major; 2, the analogy of ideas or analogous inferences; 3, analogy of two objects in one verse; 4, analogy of two objects in two verses; 5, general and special; 6, analogy of another passage; 7, the connection.

Hillel died ten years after the birth of Christ. "Ah! the tender-hearted, the pious, the disciple of Ezra," was the lament over his grave. He was the founder of a family and race of hierarchs in the wisdom and administration of the law, who, in fifteen generations (10–415 A.D.) held the dignity of nasim or "patriarchs."

SHAMMAI.

Of Shammai, Hillel's colleague, but comparitively little is known. He was a formalist of the narrowest schools, a man of a forbidding and uncompromising temper, and, in this respect, as in others, the counterpart of his illustrious companion, of whom, both in their dispositions and divisions on a multitude of rabbinical questions, he was, as we may say, the antithesis. This antithesis is especially shown in the famous controversy carried on between Hillel and

Shammai concerning the egg laid on the Sabbath, and to which reference has already been made. Very graphically does Dean Stanley describe the disputes of both these sages in the following words :

"The disputes between Hillel and Shammai turn, for the most part, on points so infinitely little that the small controversies of ritual and dogma which have vexed the soul of Christendom seem great in comparison. They are worth recording only as accounting for the obscurity into which they have fallen, and also because churches of all ages and creeds may be instructed by the reflection that questions of the modes of eating and cooking and walking and sitting seemed as important to the teachers of Israel— on the eve of their nation's destruction, and of the greatest religious revolution that the world has seen—as the questions of dress or posture, or modes of appointment, or verbal formulas have seemed to contending schools of Christian theology." (*l.c.*, III. 501).

Though each gave often a decision the reverse of the other, yet by a sort of fiction in the practice of schools, these contrary decisions were held to be co-ordinate in authority, and, if we may believe the Talmud, were confirmed as of like authority by a *bath-kol* (a voice from heaven): "Both these and these speak the words of the living God."

This saying passed for law, and the contradictory sayings of both these rabbins are perpetuated in the Talmud to this day. And although both were rabbinically one, yet their disciples formed two irreconcilable parties, like the Scotists and Thomists of the middle ages, whose mutual dissidence manifested itself not only in the strife of words, but also in that of blows, and in some cases in that of bloodshed. So great was the antagonism between them that it was said that "Elijah the Tishbite would never be able to reconcile the disciples of Shammai and Hillel." Even in Jerome's times this antagonism between these two schools lasted, for he reports (*Comment in Esaiam* viii. 14,) that the Jews regarded them with little favor, for Shammai's school they called the " Scatterer " and Hillel's the " Profane," because they deteriorated and corrupted the law with their inventions.

The recorded principle of Shammai was: " Let thy repetition of the law be at a fixed hour "—which according to Stanley was " the hard and fast line by which his disciples were to be bound down, as by an inexorable necessity, to the punctual reading of the Sacred Book, as of a breviary, at hours never to be lost sight of "—" speak little, but do what thou hast to do with a cheerful countenance " (Aboth I, 15). " That voice," says Dean Stanley, " has a touching accent, as though he felt that the frequent professions and austere demeanor which were congenial to his natural disposition might perchance prove a stumbling-block to the cause which was dear to him."

The age of Hillel was, in many respects, the most distinguished. It was also that in which he appeared and came

> " To heal all the wounds of the world,
> The Son of the Virgin was born."

Most, if not all the Rabbins, who lived at that period, as Papias, Ben Bagh Bagh, Jochanan the Horonite and others, must have witnessed His advent, have taught during His life-time, " and had a more or less direct share in His rejection and death. Considering the state of the synagogue, can we still wonder at this? Could their pride and exclusiveness, their wrangling and learning, their religious zeal and ardor, have found satisfaction in the life, the work, or the teaching of Jesus of Nazereth," which

were in direct antagonism with their own ?
Both systems could not co-exist. Either He
or they must go down. His ascendency
would be their undoing.

GAMALIEL I.

The next in the presidency was Hillel's
grandson, Gamaliel I., *the Elder* (A.D. 30–51),
the teacher of the Apostle Paul, and the
same who gave the temperate advice which
led to the suspension of the persecution of
the early church. Among Jewish doctors
Gamaliel had been honored with the title
of *Rabban*, "our teacher." As Aquinas
among the school-men was called *Doctor An-
gelicus*, and Bonaventura *Doctor Seraphicus*,
so Gamaliel was called the " Beauty of the
Law "(כבוד התורה). He is said to have been the
thirty-fifth receiver of the traditions from
Mount Sinai; and he added to all the am-
plitude of Hebrew law a large acquaintance
with Gentile literature ; the study of Greek
being connived at, in his case, by his
rabbinical brethren, on the plea of his having
need of that language in diplomatic trans-
actions with the secular government. A
master also in the astronomy of that day,
he could test, it is said, the witnesses for
the new moon, by a chart of the lunar mo-
tions he had constructed for the purpose.
His astronomic skill was employed also in
the rectification of the Jewish calendar. It
is recorded that he delighted much in the
study of nature, and in the beautiful in all
its manifestations. " In short, Gamaliel appears to have been a man of an enlarged
and refined mind, and no very stringent
Pharisee, though connected with the sect."
Casual notices of him in the Talmud make
this evident. Thus, he had a figure en-

graved upon his seal, a thing of which no
strict Pharisee could approve. Nor could
such an one have permitted himself to enter
a public bath in which was a statue of
Aphrodite. But this Gamaliel is reported to
have done at Ptolemais, justifying himself by
the argument that the bath had been built
before the statue was there, that the building had been erected not as a temple, but
as a bath, and as such he used it (Mishna
Aboda Sarah, iii., 5).

The attitude assumed by Gamaliel toward
the Christians has induced others to surmise
that this distinguished Rabbi was at heart a
believer in Jesus, and that he was openly
baptized before his death by St. Peter and
St. Paul, together with his son Gamaliel and
Nicodemus. From Graetz, *Geschichte der
Juden* iv. p. 437, we learn, that in a church at
Pisa, the tomb of Gamaliel the Elder was
shown, who was converted to Christianity,
and whom the church canonized. The
tomb, which contains the remains of many
such converts, bears the following inscription:

" Hoc in Sarcophago requiescunt corpora sacra
Sanctorum. . . . Sanctus Gamaliel. . . .
Gamaliel divi Pauli didascalus olim,
Doctor et excellens Israelita fuit,
Concilii magni fideique peromnia cultor."

But these notices are altogether irreconcilable with the esteem and respect in which
he was held in later times by the Jewish
rabbins, who never doubted the soundness
of his creed, but who, on the contrary, said
that at his decease "the glory of the law
had ceased, and purity and abstinence died
away" (*Mishna Sota* ix. 15). "Indeed," as
Mr. Etheridge well observed :—

"The two systems of Judaism and Christianity had now
become so strongly defined, as to render neutrality in the

case of a man so publicly known impossible. Jews and Christians, as much, could no longer coalesce. One cause was the antagonism of Christianity to the corruptions with which Rabbinism had damaged the Jewish system. For while the new communion had accepted all the truths, and retained all the permanent realities of the O. T. dispensation, it speedily, and in the spirit inculcated by the teachings of its Divine Founder, disengaged itself from the human and oppressive additions of the Sopherim. But as these mischievous corruptions had become the religion, so to speak, of the mass of the people, as well as an effective apparatus of government in the practice of their spiritual rulers, the propagators of the new faith found it extremely difficult to make a favorable impression on the nation at large. Then the Catholicity of the evangelical dispensation was opposed to the favorite ideas of the Jewish mind. The elect people identified with the reign of the expected Deliverer their own ascendency over a vassal world; but the Gospel proclaimed the advent of the Messiah of all nations, whose sceptre was to shed equal blessings on all the tribes of the earth. The Saviour of our race had been manifested, not to aggrandize a sect, but to redeem a world; to be a light to illumine the Gentiles, as well as to be the glory of his people Israel."

The recorded theological principle of Gamaliel expresses his adherence to traditionalism and his abhorrence of Pharisaical wrangling and hypocritical over-scrupulousness. It is: "Procure thyself a teacher, avoid being in doubt and do not accustom thyself to give tithes by guess." (*Aboth*, I., 16.)

SIMEON.

Gamaliel was succeeded by his son Simeon (50–70 A.D.). The authentic notices of him are very few. We get a glimpse or two of him in the storm which was then so fiercely raging in Jerusalem. As the resolute opponent of the Zealots, he took an active part in the political struggles, whose convulsions hastened the ruin of the state. He also took an active part in the defence of Jerusalem, and fell, one of the many victims of the national struggle. Josephus (*Life*, section 38) says of him: "This Simon

3

was of the city of Jerusalem, and of a very noble family, of the sect of the Pharisees, which are supposed to excel others in the accurate knowledge of the laws of their country. He was a man of great wisdom and reason, and capable of restoring public affairs by his prudence, when they were in an ill posture." His recorded maxim is: " The world exists by virtue of three things —viz., truth, justice and peace ; as it is written, Truth and the judgment of peace shall be in your gates " (*Aboth,* I. 18). He also belongs to the ten teachers who were called הרוני מלכות " the killed for the king-dom," and their death is commemorated on the 25th day of Sivan, for which day a fast is ordained.

With the destruction of Jerusalem a new epoch commenced not only in the history of the Jewish people, but more especially in the development of Jewish scholasticism. The seat of learning was removed to Jabne, or Jamnia, and the most prominent teacher of the new school was

JOHANAN BEN SAKKAI AND HIS SUCCESSORS.

He had escaped from Jerusalem by being carried on a bier as one who had died. When he had reached the Roman camp, he was welcomed by Vespasian and allowed to proffer a request. Rabbi Johanan is said to have first conciliated the general's favor by predicting his future accession to the purple. Then instead of asking any personal favors, he only requested permission, to establish a school at Jabne. The request was granted, and Johanan now settled with his disciples at Ramla, near Jabne, to await there the issue of events. When tidings of the destruction of the Temple reached them, he comforted

his disciples, and as the head of the school
he adapted Judaism to the altered political
circumstances.   Jabne was substituted for
Jerusalem, certain ordinances were discon-
tinued or slightly altered, and certain prayers
or good works substituted for sacrifices, and
the change was effected without leaving any
trace of violent revolution.   The branch of
theology in which Johanan excelled, was
that known as the Haggada.   Of his disciples the Mishna mentions *Eliezer ben Hyrcanus, Joshua ben Hananja, José, the Priest,
Simeon ben Nathanael, Eleasar ben Arach.*
The first two are the best known and most·
prominent.

Rabbi Johanan died on his bed in the arms·
of his disciples.   His dying words were:
" Fear God even as you fear men."   His disciples seemed astonished.   He added : " He
who would commit a sin, first looks round to
discover whether any man sees him ; so take
ye heed, that God's all-seeing eye see not the
sinful thought in your heart."   There is another of his last words.   His disciples addressed him : " Rabbi, light of Israel, thou·
strong rock, right-hand pillar, why dost thou
weep?"   He answered them : " If they were
about to lead me before a king of flesh and
blood, who is to-day here and to-morrow in·
the grave, who if he were angry with me, his
anger would not last forever ; if he put me
in bondage, his bondage would not be everlasting ; and if he condemned me to death,
that death would not be eternal ; whom I
could soothe with words and bribe with
money ; yet, even in these circumstances, I
should weep.   But now I am about to appear before the awful majesty of the King of
Kings, before the Holy and Blessed One,
who is, and who liveth forever, whose just
anger may be eternal, who may doom me to

eternal punishment.   Should he condemn
me, it will be to death without further hope.
Nor can I pacify Him with words, nor bribe
Him with money.   There are two roads before me, one leading to Paradise, the other
to Hell, and I know not by which of these I
go—should I not weep?"   We see thus, in
Johanan's life and death, a signal instance of
the unsatisfactory character of Rabbinism.
Even this famous man was made to feel and
exemplify, that "by the deeds of the law
there shall no flesh be justified." [1]

Johanan's successor as head of the school
at Jabne was Gamaliel II., son of Simon, and
grandson of Gamaliel I. (about 90–110 A.D.).
He exercised the prerogative of his office in
the most despotic manner, silencing by excommunication those whom he could not
convince by arguments.   This attempt at
spiritual tyranny, however, ultimately issued
in his own humiliation and final deposition.
Gamaliel, after having seen his error, and
having implored the pardon of his colleagues,
was again re-instated.   With a few exceptions, Gamaliel was an adherent of the school
of Hillel, and in legal matters, acted accordingly.

The two most famous cotemporaries of
Gamaliel were Rabbi Joshua ben Hananja and
Rabbi Eliezer ben Hyrcanus, both disciples

---

1. Lightfoot in the spirit of his time and opinion says insultingly:
" Oh, the wretched and failing faith of a Pharisee in the hour of
death " (*Academiæ Jafnensis Historiæ Fragmenta.* 1 p 446. ed.
Pitman). A modern writer says: '' What a contrast is presented in
the history of a disciple of the celebrated Rabbi Gamaliel. one who
had profited above many of his equals in age in the Jew's religion,
being more exceedingly zealous of the traditions of his fathers.
He had them cast off; he had counted them loss for Christ, and now,
in the prospect of eternity, exultingly exclaims : " Henceforth there
is laid up for me a crown of righteousness, which the Lord the
Righteous Judge shall give me at that day," and in the animating
prospect of the Redeemer's triumph over death, leads on the
Christian hosts with the exultant shout, ' O death where is thy
sting?   O grave where is thy victory?   Thanks be to God which
gives us the victory through Jesus, the Messiah, our Lord." (Reynolds, *Six Lectures on the Jews*, London, 1847.)

of Johanan ben Sakkai. Only the former seems to have been on friendly terms with Gamaliel, not so the latter, who according to tradition has been excommunicated by the patriarch, his own brother-in-law. Eliezer had a school at Lydda, but upon his excommunication he retired to Cæsarea where he died about 117 A.D.

When Gamaliel died, the temporary administration of spiritual affairs devolved on Rabbi Joshua. Like Eliezer, he, too, had opened a college at Lydda after the decease of Rabbi Johanan ben Sakkai. He trained a number of most intelligent pupils, of whom some became distinguished for attainments in the Halakha. On account of his mild and liberal views on all theological and general questions, he was probably the only Jewish doctor who not only enjoyed the full confidence of the Roman authorities, but who also employed his influences for the advantage both of his countrymen and of their rulers.

AQIBA BEN JOSEPH.

Amongst the many pupils of Rabbi Joshua, none became so renowned as Aqiba ben Joseph, the systematizer of Rabbinism, the Thomas Aquinas of the Oral Law. The old Jewish writers have embellished their biographies with such a variety of fables, as to make it difficult to give a substantially true account of the persons who were the subjects of them. Aqiba, who flourished about 110– 135 A. D., studied under three different teachers, and derived from each a claim of peculiar distinction. From Nahum of Gimso he had learned those exegetical principles which attached such celebrity to the name of that theologian. [1] Eliezer ben Hyrcanus had probably laid the foundation of his more solid learning, while Rabbi Joshua ben Hananjah initiated him in the mysteries of the Kabbalah. Aqiba may be considered as the only systematic Tanaïte. Thus he arranged the different halakhas first after their contents —which division was called *masichta* or *textus*—and then enumerated them in such a manner as to assist the memory of the student. Besides his arrangement of the Mishna, which was called the Mishna of Rabbi Aqiba, he also grounded its text upon Scripture, or at least made the first systematic and consistent attempt toward it. But more than the enumeration or exposition of the halakha, his peculiar and novel method of expounding the Scriptures fascinated his hearers. " He founded a science of casuistry to which the plain meaning of the Written Law became of less and less importance;" he opened ways for the exercise of ingenuity, and its results were made subservient to the interests of traditionalism.

Thus Nahum of Gimso had declared some particles in the Scriptures as significant, but Aqiba went beyond that, declaring that every *sentence, word,* and *particle* in the Bible must have its use and meaning. He denied that mere rhetorical figures, repetitions, or accumulations occurred in the Bible. *Every* word, syllable, and letter, which was not absolutely requisite to express the meaning which it was desired to convey, must, he maintained, serve some ulterior purpose, and be intended to indicate a special meaning. Rabbi Aqiba reduced his views to a system. The seven exegetical principles of Hillel were enlarged

---

1. Nahum explained that some particles were excluding, whilst others were including. This method was called " the rule of extension and restriction " (*ribbuj u-miut*).

into forty-nine, which were strictly applied to
every possible case, not only in hagadic interpretations, but also in the study of the halakha, in the highest judicial procedures, and
even as groundwork for fresh inferences.
Sometimes, however, these principles were
put to a severe test. Thus, on one occasion,
they were applied to the text, " Thou shalt
honor the Lord thy God," in which a particle not absolutely requisite was discovered.
One of Aqiba's pupils objected that it might
be inferred that some one else besides God
was to be supremely reverenced, but Aqiba
removed his doubts by replying that the particle in question was intended to point to
the law, which ought to be honored next to
the Lord.

Rabbi Aqiba's method was hailed as the
commencement of a new period. His cotemporaries yielded to the most extravagant
transports of delight. Thus Rabbi Tarphon,
heretofore surpassing Rabbi Aqiba, addressed
him respectfully : " He that forsakes thee, forsakes eternal life ; what tradition had forgotten thou hast restored by the method of
interpretation." Rabbi Joshua, Aqiba's former teacher, although wary on these subjects,
could not repress a wish that Johanan ben
Sakkai had been alive to witness the firm
establishment of the halakha. In their extravagance, the rabbis went so far as to as-
sert that Aqiba had discovered many things
of which even Moses was ignorant.

Aqiba's great maxim was " that everything is ordained of heaven for the best."
With this axiom on his lips, he was riding
with some of his followers near the ruins of
Jerusalem. They burst into tears at the
melancholy sight. for, to heighten their grief,
they beheld a jackal prowling upon the hill
of the Temple. Aqiba only observed that

the very success of the idolatrous Romans,
as they fulfilled the words of the prophets,
were grounds of loftier hopes for the people
of God. The end of these lofty hopes must
have severely tried the resignation of Aqiba.
He was yet in the zenith of his fame, though
now nearly 120 years old; he is said, also,
by some, to have been the head of the Sanhedrin when Bar Cochab, or Coziba, announced his pretensions as the Messiah.
Aqiba had but lately returned from a visit,
or from a flight, to his Mesopotamian brethren; and whether the state of affairs at
Nahardea and Nisibis had awakened his
hopes and inflamed a noble jealousy, which
induced him to risk any hazard to obtain
equal independence for his brethren in
Judea, or whether there was any general and
connected plan for the reassertion of Jewish
liberty, he threw himself at once into the
party of the heaven-inspired insurgent.
" Behold," said the hoary enthusiast, in an
assembly of the listening people, " the Star
that is come out of Jacob ; the days of the
redemption are at hand." " Aqiba," said the
more cautious Rabbi Johanan, "the grass
will spring from thy jawbone, and yet the
son of David will not have come." Without
narrating the events of this insurrection,
which proved as abortive as former ones, we
will only state that it was again on the fatal
9th day of Ab (August), the anniversary of
the double destruction in Jerusalem, that
the fortified town of Bether fell, the son of
the star, Bar Cochba, was killed, and his
head carried in triumph to the Roman camp.

Among those who were destined to die
was also Aqiba, the brave martyr of an
ignoble cause. " Had " says Farrar, " Aqiba
been trained in truer and nobler methods,
he might not have committed the gross

error of confusing a Barkoziba with a Bar-
kokhba—the 'son of a lie' with the 'son
of a star.'" Amongst those who opposed
Aqiba's principles was none more distinguished by birth, personal character, or
learning, than Rabbi *Ismael*, who lived in
the south of Palestine, not far from the
Idumean boundaries, at a place called
Kephar Aziz. The remarkable part of his
life to us is the system of interpretation
which he laid down in opposition to that of
Aqiba. In opposition to the latter, Ismael
maintained that the Bible, being written in
human language, uses expressions in their
common acceptation, that many of the repetitions and parallelisms are simply designed
to render the style more rhetorical, and
powerful, and cannot, therefore, without
violation of the laws of language, be adduced in support of legal deductions. Accordingly he laid down thirteen exegetical
rules, which are called the thirteen rules of
Rabbi Ismael, by which alone the Scriptures
are to be interpreted, and which are as follows: 1. Inference from minor to major; 2.
The comparison of words or ideas; 3. Building of the father, or the chief law, from one
verse, and the chief law from two verses · 4.
General and special; 5. Special and general; 6. General, special, and general; 7. A
general subject which requires a special one,
and a special one which requires a general
subject for mutual explanation; 8. When a
special law is enacted for something which
has already been comprised in a general law,
it shows that it is also to be applied to the
whole class; 9. When a subject included in
a general description is excepted from it
or another enactment, whilst it remains in
all other respects like it, it is excepted to be
alleviated, but not aggravated; 10. When a

subject included in a general description is
excepted from it for another enactment,
whilst it is also not like it in other respects,
it is excepted both to be alleviated and aggravated, *i c.*, its connection with the general
law entirely ceases; 11. If a subject included in a general description has been excepted from it for the enactment of a new
and opposite law, it cannot be restored again
to the general class unless the Bible itself
expressly restores it; 12. The sense of an
indefinite statement must either be deter-
mined from its connection, or from the form
and tendency of the statement itself; 13.
When two statements seem to contradict
each other, a third statement will reconcile
them.

Rabbinic Judaism regarded these rules of
such an importance that it made it obliga-
tory for every Jew to recite them in the
morning-prayer; hence these rules may be
found in every Jewish prayer-book.

CONTEMPORARIES OF AQIBA.

Ismael, who died in the year 121 A.D., is
also the reputed author of a number of
works. The most important of these are an
allegorical commentary on Exodus, called
Mechilta.[1] The Mechilta is composed of
nine tractates, subdivided into sections, and
treats on select sections of Exodus in the
following order: The first tract treats on
Exodus xii. 1–13, in eighteen sections; the
second on xiii. 17–xiv. 31 in six sections; the
third on xv. 1–21 in ten sections; the fourth
on xv. 22–xvii. 7 in seven sections; the fifth
on xvii. 8–xviii. 27 in four sections; the sixth

---

1. Best edition by Weiss, Vienna, 1865, and by M. Friedman, *ibid.*
1870. A Latin translation is found in Ugolini's *Thesaurus Antiq-*
uitatum, vol. xiv. (Venice, 1752).

on xix. 1–xx. 22 in eleven sections; the seventh on xxi. 1–xxii. 23 in eighteen sections; the eighth on xxii. 23–xxiii. 19 in two sections; and the ninth on xxxi. 12–17, xxxv. 1–3, in two sections. Besides the Mechilta, some cabbalistic works are ascribed to Ismael.

Prominent among Aqiba's contemporaries was Rabbi Tarphon,[1] who belonged to a sacerdotal family, and whose recorded maxim was : " The day is short, the labor vast ; but the laborers are slothful, though the reward is great, and the Master presseth for dispatch. It is not incumbent upon thee to complete the work, and yet thou art not at liberty to be idle about it. If thou hast studied the law much, great reward will be given thee ; for faithful is thy employer, who will award to thee the hire of thy labor, and be aware that the award of the righteous will be in the future which is to come."[2] The manner in which he applied the Scripture is best illustrated by the following : When some one told him something intellectual, he used to say, " A knop and a flower in one branch " (Exod. xxv. 33); but when the tale was not according to his taste, he used to say, " My son shall not go down with you." [3]

Another Tanaïte of the same period was Jose the Galilean, known as the author of thirty-two rules, whereby the Bible is to be interpreted.[4]

As soon as the war had terminated a Jewish synod was convoked at Ussa or Usha, and *Simon ben Gamaliel II.*, who had escaped the sword of the Roman conqueror

---

1. Of his animosity against Christianity, we shall speak further on.
2. *Aboth*, II., 20 *seq.*
3. *Bereshith Rabba*, section 91.
4. Given in full by Pinner, Treatise *Berachoth*, fol. 20 *seq.* Compare also Brigg's *Biblical Study*, p. 301, where the principles of the methods of Ismael and Jose are summed up in the words of a modern Jewish writer.

from the slaughter at Bether, was elected as
the spiritual head of the college of rabbis
(about 140–160 A.D.). Of prominent teachers
we mention *Rabbi Nathan*, the author of the
celebrated " Sayings " which go by his name ;
Joseph ben Halafta, who died in 150 A.D.,
author of an historical work entitled " Seder
Olam " ; *Juda ben Ilaï*, surnamed " the Just,"
who made the book of Leviticus his special
study, and is considered as the first author
of the Midrashic work entitled *Sifre*, which
was afterwards more fully elaborated ; *Simeon
ben Jochai*, the master of the Kabbala, the legendary author of the Zohar, whose political
views became the source of political troubles,
which finally resulted in the overthrow of
the school of Jabne ; and finally *Rabbi Meïr*,
the casuist, whose permanent merit consisted in continuing the labors of his master
Aqiba in the arrangement of the halakha.
This he carried to a stage further by dividing according to their contents the traditions, which had hitherto been only strung
together according to their number.   In this
respect the patriarch's son, Juda, was much
indebted to his tuition.   Simon ben Gamaliel
II. was succeeded by

RABBI JUDA THE HOLY.

This rabbi, called "the Holy,' or "the
Prince," or " Our Master," or simply and
emphatically by the mere title *Rabbi* as
though no other were worthy to be compared with him, was by far the most distinguished of that race since Hillel the
Great, and the last truly distinguished Jewish patriarch of Palestine.   Born about the
year 136, on the very day on which Rabbi
Aqiba suffered martyrdom, he attracted attention at an early age, and when his father

died, he followed him in the presidency of
the Sanhedrin.

Juda inherited to a remarkable extent the
two qualities of his predecessors, acuteness
and ambition. The vast riches which the
family had accumulated, and the learning
and originality which favorably distinguished
him from his father Simon, enabled him to
carry out the hierarchical designs of the latter, which had now almost become the traditional policy of the family of Hillel. Juda
soon obtained the sole right of ordination,
and it was enacted that none but regularly
ordained teachers were in future to pro-
nounce on any religious question—a rule
which, as will easily be inferred, excluded all
but the patriarch's favorites from places of
influence or authority. His residence, and
that of the Sanhedrin, was at first at Beth-
Shearim (the modern Turan), and afterwards
at Sepphoris, a place chosen for its salubri-
ous air, and where he died in 200.

His most lasting and important measure,
whereby he achieved the greatest claim to
renown, was the collection of the Mishna.
" Down to his time," says Farrar, " the traditions of the Fathers had never been put
into writing. It had been a rule of the Rabbis that what had been delivered orally was
only to be retained by the memory. That
rule was founded on the principle that circumstances change, and therefore that oral
decisions ought not to be regarded as final
precedents. By this time, however, it had
become an impossibility to retain a mass of
precedents so heterogeneous and so immense as those which had been accumulated
from the days of Ezra to those of Aqiba.
Accordingly *Rabbi Juda*, for the first time,
committed to writing the Oral Law arranged
under the six orders of Hillel's classification.

His compilation was called "the Mishna,"
"learning," or "Repetition." It acquired
an influence truly secular. It summed up
the labors of four centuries. The Oral Law
had been recognized by Ezra; had become
important in the days of the. Maccabees;
had been supported by Pharisaism; nar-
rowed by the school of Shammai, codified
by the school of Hillel, systematized by R.
Aqiba, placed on a logical basis by R.
Ismael, exegetically amplified by R. Eliezer,
and constantly enriched by successive rabbis
and their schools. *Rabbi* put the coping-
stone to the immense structure. Thence-
forth the Mishna moulded the entire theology and philosophy of Judaism. The publication of tradition put an end to the independent energy of the Halakha, and closed
the long succession of the Tanaim. The
Mishna became the bond of Jewish nationality. It put an end to the Patriarchate
of which it was the child. It completed the
"hedge about the law," which henceforth
neither persecution nor dispersion could destroy, and through which neither Hellenism,
nor Sadduceeism, nor Alexandrianism, nor
Gnosticism, nor Christianity, nor the Renais-
sance, nor the Reformation, nor modern
skepticism, down to the days of Moses Men-
delssohn, could break their way. This
strange collection of completed and dead
"decisions," being treated as of divine authority, superseded, all but entirely, the
Scriptures on which they professed to have
been based. The bold initiative of *Rabbi*
stamped on Judaism a character singularly
dry and juristic, and laid upon the necks of
all Talmudic Jews a yoke unspeakably more
empty and indefinitely more galling than
that of which St. Peter had complained even
in the days when the observance of Mosaism

had not yet been rendered impossible by the fiat of history, which is the manifest will of God."[1]

THE MISHNA.

The Mishna, which a Jewish historian has pronounced a work, the possession of which by the Hebrew nation compensated them for the loss of their ancestral country; a book which constitutes a kind of homestead for the Jewish mind, an intellectual and moral fatherland for a people who, in their long lasting discipline of suffering, are exiles and aliens in all the nations of the earth, is composed of different elements. Besides the elucidation of the fundamental texts of the Mosaic laws, and their application to an endless variety of particular cases and circumstances not mentioned in them, it contains the decisions of the sages and of individuals, decisions demanded by emergencies and universal principles under which a multitude of particular cases may be provided for. These manifold materials Juda or Rabbi arranged under six general classes, called *Sedarim* or " Orders." The *first* relating to the productions of the earth, as forming the staple sustenance of human life, is called *Zeraim*, *i.e.*, " seeds." The *second* referring to times and seasons, involving the religious observance of years and days, feasts and festivals, is called *Moëd* or " Festival Solemnity." The *third*, called *Nashim* or " Women," deals with the institution of marriage, which lies at the, basis of the system of human society. The *fourth* called *Nezikin* or " Injuries " relates to civil controversies, and treats of the rights of persons and things. The *fifth* com-

---

1. *History of Interpretation*, p. 80 *seq.*

prises laws and regulations regarding the
service and worship of God, upon the pro-
visions of the Levitical ritual, or things
consecrated, and is called *Kodashim*, *i.e.*,
Consecrations. The *sixth* exhibits the prescriptions requisite to the maintenance or
recovery of personal purity, according to the
Levitical ideas, and is called *Tohoroth*, *i.e.*,
" Purifications."

The regulations thus generally classified
are further arranged under a multitude of
subsidiary topics ; each Seder being divided
into a number of tracts or treatises, called
masiktoth, and these again subdivided into
Perakim, *i.e.*, chapters, and each chapter
again into *Mishnioth* or paragraphs. The
whole is called *Shas*. The following is an
analysis of the contents of each tractate of
the six orders :

I. SEDER ZERAIM (Seed). This Seder
contains the following eleven tractates :
1. *Berachoth*, or the treatise of blessings,
and speaks in nine chapters of the daily
prayers and thanksgivings, etc.,—(*a*,) the first
chapter treats of the time when the Shema-
prayer is to be recited in the morning and
evening, of the position of the body at
prayers, and the benedictions to be said
respectively (5 sections); (*b*,) the second
speaks of the sections and order of the
Shema-prayer, or how the voice is to be
used in saying the prayer, and of the occasions which exempt from prayer (8 sections);
(*c*,) the third points out such as are exempted from prayer (6 sections); (*d*,) the
fourth treats of the time during which
prayers may be said, whether the *Shemoneh
Esre* (*i.e.*, 18 benedictions) are to be said in
an abbreviated manner ; of prayer as an
opus operatum, of praying in dangerous

places, and of the additional prayer (7 sections); (*e*,) the fifth refers to the outer and inner position at prayer; of prayer for rain; of the prayer on Sabbath evening; of the ministers of the congregation and mistakes in prayer (5 sections); (*f*,) the sixth recites the different blessings to be said for fruits of the tree and the earth, wine and bread; for wine before and after meals; of the sitting and lying at the table; of blessings for the main meals and water (8 sections); (*g*,) the seventh expatiates on blessings pronounced conjointly; with whom a union for such a purpose may be entered upon; the form of prayer to be used in accordance with the number of persons, of different companies (5 sections); (*h*,) the eighth shows the differences between the schools of Hillel and Shammai concerning the washing of hands and the blessing at meals (8 sections); (*i*,) the ninth names the prayer to be said at beholding signs and wonders, at the building of a new house, and treats of prayers offered in vain, of prayers at the leaving and going into a city; of the praising of God for the good as well as for the evil; how to approach the Temple mountain; of the using of the name of God at salutations (5 sections).

II. PEAH, OR THE CORNER OF THE FIELD, treats in eight chapters, of the field corners, gleanings, etc., to be left to the poor, etc.,— (*a*,) in the first chapter we read of the measure of the Peah, where, of what, and how large it must be given, and how long the fruit is exempted from tithe (6 sections); (*b*,) the second treats of how fields and trees as to the Peah may be separated from each other (8 sections); (*c*,) tells us how large a field must be of which Peah must be given (11 sections); (*d*,) shows how the Peah must

be given (11 sections); (*e,*) tells what belongs to the poor, and treats of the bunch
left through forgetfulness (8 sections); (*f,*)
speaks of what may be regarded as a bunch
left through forgetfulness, and what not
(11 sections); (*g,*) treats of the same matter
concerning olive-trees ; on the right of the
poor in the vineyard (8 sections); (*h,*) speaks
of how long the right of the poor lasts;
what constitutes the poor, and who is not
entitled to the right of the poor (9 sections).

III. DEMAÏ, OR DOUBTFUL treats in seven
chapters of fruits about which some doubts
may be raised whether tithes should be
paid for them or not, viz., (*a,*) which fruits
are exempted from the rights of Demaï
how the Demaï tithe differs from other
tithes, and as to the rights of Demaï fruits
(4 sections); (*b,*) who may be regarded a
strict Israelite, and to whom the performance of the Demaï law belongs at buying
and selling; (*c,*) who may reserve Demaï
for eating, and that nothing should be
given away untithed (6 sections); (*d,*) how a
man may be believed concerning the tithes
(7 sections); how the tithe is to be given
from Demaï (11 sections); (*e,*) what to do at
the renting of a field, at the pressing in
company, and of the fruits in Syria (12
sections); (*f,*) how to act with such as are
not believed concerning the tithes; how to
separate the tithes in divers cases; and
what must be taken into account when
tithed and untithed fruits are mixed up
(8 sections).

IV. KILAYIM, OR MIXTURES treats, in
nine chapters, of the prohibited mingling of
fruit and grain crops on the same field, etc.,
viz. (*a,*) which kinds of fruits, trees, and
animals are Kilayim, and how to graft and
plant (9 sections); (*b,*) what to do when two

kinds of seed are mixed, or in case of sowing another kind on a field already sown, or in case of making beds of different corn in one field (11 sections); (*c,*) of beds, their division; of cabbage and its distance (7 sections); (*d* and *e,*) of vineyards and their Kilayim (9 and 8 sections); (*f,*) of the rights of a vine raised on an espalier (9 sections); (*g,*) of the layering of vines, spreading of vines, etc., (8 sections); (*h,*) in how far Kilayim are forbidden among animals, in yoking together as well as in copulating, and what to do with bastards and some other animals (6 sections); (*i,*) of Kilayim in garments, especially of the mixture of wool and flax; of clothing—merchants and tailors; of felt and woven letters, etc. (10 sections).

V. SHEBÜTH OR THE SABBATICAL YEAR, in ten chapters: (*a,*) of fields with trees, and how long they may be cultivated in the sixth year (8 sections); (*b,*) of open fields, and what may be done in them till the beginning of the seventh year (10 sections); (*c,*) of manuring the field; of breaking stones and pulling down walls (10 sections); (*d,*) of cutting and pruning trees; from what time on it is permitted to eat of the fruits of the seventh year which have grown by themselves (10 sections); (*e,*) concerning the white fig and summer onions; which farm utensils cannot be sold and lent (9 sections); (*f,*) of the difference of countries concerning the seventh year, and what fruits cannot be taken outside of the country (6 sections); (*g,*) what things are subject to the right of the seventh year (7 sections); (*h,*) what use may be made of fruits which have grown by themselves; what must be observed at their sale and the proceeds thereof; how they are to be gathered (11 sections); (*i,*) of the fruits which may be bought, and of storing away the preserved fruits (9 sections); (*j*,) of the remittance of debts (9 sections).

VI. TERUMOTH OR OBLATIONS, relates in eleven chapters, to the heave offering; (*a*,) what persons can give the Terumoth, and of which fruits; and of giving the Terumoth not according to number, measure and weight (10 sections); (*b*,) the Terumoth cannot be given from the pure for the impure; of distinguishing whether something was done purposely or by mistake; and that one kind of fruit can supply the Terumoth of another (6 sections); (*c*,) in which cases the Terumoth must be given a second time; how to determine the Terumah; of the Terumah of a Gentile (9 sections); (*d* and *e*,) of the quantity of the large Terumah: in which cases common fruit becomes not medumma (*i.e.*, is to be given entirely as Terumah), in spite of having been mixed with Terumah (13 and 9 sections); (*f*,) of the restitution of the Terumah, when a person has eaten thereof by mistake (5 sections); (*g*,) when a person eats thereof with intention (7 sections); (*h*,) of the care that a Terumah get neither unclean nor poisoned (12 sections); (*i*,) what is to be done in case Terumah has been sown (7 sections); (*j*,) how common fruits by the mere taste can become Terumah fruit (12 sections); (*k*,) how the oil of a Terumah cannot be burned, when the priest cannot enjoy its light (10 sections).

VII. MAASEROTH, OR TITHES, due to the Levites, in five chapters; (*a*,) of the kinds of fruits subject to tithes, and from what time on they are due (8 sections) (*b*,) of exceptions (8 sections); (*c*,) where fruits become tithable (10 sections); (*d*,) of preserving, picking out, and other cases exempted from tithes (6 sections); (*e,*) of removing of plants, of buying and selling : of wine and seed that cannot be tithed (8 sections).

VIII. MAASER SHENI, OR SECOND TITHE, which the Levites had to pay out of their tenth to the priests, in five chapters, (*a,*) that this tenth cannot be disposed of in any way (7 sections); (*b,*) only things necessary for eating, drinking, and anointing, can be bought for the money of the tenth ; what to do when tenth money must be exchanged (10 sections); (*c,*) fruits of the second tenth, while once in Jerusalem, cannot be taken out again (13 sections) ; (*d,*) what must be observed at the price of the tenth, and how money and that which is found must be regarded (12 sections); (*e,*) of a vineyard in its fourth year, the fruits of which are equally regarded as the fruits of the second tenth ; and how the *biur*, or taking away of the tenth, is performed in a solemn manner according to Deut. xxvi. 13 *seq.* (15 sections.)

IX. CHALLAH OR DOUGH, refers to the cake which the women were required to bring of kneaded dough to the priest, in four chapters : (*a,*) which fruits are subject to challah (9 sections) ; (*b* and *c,*) of special cases which need a more precise definition concerning challah, and of the quantity of meal and its challah (8 and 10 sections); (*d,*) of counting together of different fruits, and the different rights of countries concerning Challah (11 sections).

X. ORLAH, *lit.* FORESKIN, of the forbidden fruits of the trees in Palestine during the first three years of their growth, in three chapters ; (*a,*) which trees are subject to the law of Orlah and which not (9 sections); (*b,*) what to do in case of fruits of Orlah or Kilayim being mixed with other fruits ; of the law concerning leaven, spices, and meal;

what to do in case of holy and unholy, or Chollin, having been mixed up (17 sections); (*c,*) how the same law also concerns colors for dyeing purposes, and the fire used for cooking; and what is to be observed concerning the difference of countries (9 sections).

XI. BIKKURIM OR FIRST FRUITS, in four chapters: (*a,*) who is not entitled to offer the first fruits, or who can offer them without observing the formula prescribed (Deut. xxvi., 3); of what and when they are to be offered or repaid (11 sections); (*b*) of the difference of the first fruits of the Terumah and the second tenth, especially of the pomegranate at the Feast of Tabernacles; of blood of men and of the animal Coi (probably a bastard of buck and roe), which must be distinguished from all animals (11 sections); (*c,*) of the ceremonies to be observed at bringing the first fruits to Jerusalem and their rights (12 sections); (*d,*) of the hermaphrodite (5 sections). This chapter is Boraitha, or addition to the second chapter, and is wanting where *only* the Mishna is printed.

II. SEDER MOËD (FESTIVE SOLEMNITY).

This *Seder*, one of the most interesting, consists of twelve tractates:

XII. *Shabbath,* containing twenty-four chapters, treats of the laws relating to the Sabbath, with respect to lights and oil used on that day, ovens in which articles of food were warmed on the Sabbath, and the dress of men and women used on the same day. It also enumerates thirty-nine kinds of work, by each of which, separately, the guilt of Sabbath-breaking may be incurred. It treats of the differences between the schools of Hillel and Shammai, etc., viz. (*a,*) of removals on the Sabbath day; work to be avoided; discussion between the schools of Hillel and Shammai as to what constitutes work; work allowed (11 sections); (b,) of the lighting of a lamp; eve of the Sabbath (7 sections[1]); (c,) of different ovens, and pre- paring and warming the meat on Sabbath; of pails for retention of the dripping oil or sparks of the lamps (8 sections); (d,) of things to cover up pots to retain the heat, and of things not to cover up the pots (2 sec- tions); (e,) with what a beast is led forth or covered, especially a camel (4 sections); (f,) with what women and men may go out or not go out on the Sabbath : of various styles; of pinning the veil ; of ribbons, etc. (10 sec- tions); (g,) of how many sin-offerings a man may be responsible for under certain cir- cumstances for ignorantly trespassing against the Sabbath; the thirty-nine kinds of for- bidden work; rule and measure for things the carrying of which makes liable to a sin- offering (4 sections); (h,) of the measure of fluids; of cords, bulrushes, paper, and all possible portable things (7 sections) ; (i,) of things the carrying of which makes unclean, and of the measure of the portable things on the Sabbath day (7 sections); (j,) of different kinds of portable things ; of carry- ing living or dead men, and of many other things (6 sections) ; (k), of throwing over the street, ditch, and rock, river and land ; of the distance how far it can be thrown, and the presumable error (6 sections) ; (l,) of building, hammering, planing, boring, plough- ing, gathering wood, pruning, picking up, writing (6 sections); (m,) of weaving, sewing, cutting, washing, beating, catching game,

---

1. This chapter forms a part of the prayers prescribed for Sab- bath eve.

etc. (7 sections); (*n,*) of catching game; of making salt water, of forbidden medicines, toothache, and pains in the loins; (*o,*) of tying and untying of knots; of folding garments, and making the beds (3 sections); (*p,*) of saving things out of a conflagration; of extinguishing and covering, etc. (8 sections); (*q,*) of vessels which may be moved on the Sabbath (8 sections); (*r,*) what things may be moved for making room; of hens, calves, asses; of leading the child of an animal that calves; a woman that is to be delivered, and of a child (3 sections); (*s,*) of circumcision on the Sabbath (6 sections); (*t,*) of straining the wine; of fodder; of cleansing the crib; of straw on the beds and clothes-press (5 sections); (*u,*) of things permitted to be carried; of cleaning a pillow; the table, of picking up the crumbs; and of sponges (3 sections); (*v,*) of casks, cisterns, bathing-clothes, salves, etc.; of emetics; of setting a limb or a rupture (6 sections); (*w,*) of borrowing; of counting from a book, drawing lots, hiring laborers; of waiting at the end of a Sabbath-way; of mourning-pipes, coffin and grave which a heathen has dug; what may be done to the dead (5 sections); (*x,*) of one who is overtaken by the dusk on the road; of feeding the animals; of pumpkins and carrion; of several things permitted on the Sabbath (5 sections).

XIII. ERUBIN OR MINGLING, in ten chapters, deals with those ceremonies by which the Sabbath boundary was extended; "mingling" a whole town into one fictitious yard, so that carrying within should not be unlawful; (*a* and *b,*) concerning the entry to an ally and enclosures (10 and 6 sections); (*c,*) concerning a holyday or a Friday (9 sections); (*d,*) concerning the stepping beyond the Sabbath limit (11 sections); (*e,*) concerning the enlarging the bounds of a city (9 sections); (*f* and *g*,) concerning the neighborhood (10 and 11 sections); (*h*,) concerning what may be in a yard (11 sections); (*i*,) concerning roofs, etc., (4 sections); (*j*.) concerning some different Sabbath laws (15 sections).

XIV. PESACHIM in ten chapters, treats of the paschal festival and things connected with its celebration; (*a, b,* and *c*,) of searching for leaven; how to put it away; of the Easter-cake, and the herbs for the bitter herbs; of the care to avoid leaven (7+ 8 + 9 sections); (*d*,) of the works on the day before Easter, and what kind of works are permitted (9 sections); (*e*,) when and how to kill the Paschal lamb; of cleaning and skinning the same, and how it becomes disallowed (10 sections); (*f*,) how the Passover abrogates the command against work on the Sabbath; of the offering of festival sacrifices; of a sacrifice having been changed with another (6 sections); (*g* and *h*,) of roasting the lamb; how it becomes unclean; what to do with the remaining parts; what persons are allowed to eat it and what are not; of companies (13 and 8 sections); (*i*,) of the second Easter; of the Easter in Egypt, and divers cases when paschal lambs have been exchanged (11 sections); (*j*,) of the order at the Easter-meal after the four cups of wine which are necessary for it (9 sections).

XV. SHEKALIM, OR SHEKELS, in eight chapters, contains laws relating to the half shekel which was paid for the support of public worship (*a–d*,) how the money changers take their seat at the money tables on the 15th of Adar, where the people exchange their money; of changing and of coins used in former times of the remaining money;

how the paid shekels may be taken again from the treasury; how they are to be spent, and what to do with the balance (7+5+4+9 sections); (*e,*) of the offices of the sanctuary, and of the seals (6 sections) ; (*f,*) how often the number thirteen occurred in the sanctuary (6 sections) ; (*g,*) of money and other things which are found, when it is doubtful to whom they belong (7 sections) ; (*h,*) of other dubious things, resolution that the shekel and firstlings have ceased with the Temple (8 sections.)

XVI. YOMA, OR THE DAY OF ATONEMENT, in 8 chapters, speaks (*a,*) of the preparations of the high priest (8 sections); (*b,*) of casting lots, and the offerings (7 sections); (*c,*) of the beginning of the Day of Atonement; of bathing, washing, and dressing the high priest, and of presenting the bullocks and goats (11 sections); (*d,*) of casting the lots upon the goats, and the confession (6 sections); (*e,*) what was to be done in the Holy of Holies (7 sections); (*f,*) of sending forth the goat (8 sections); (*g,*) what the high-priest was meanwhile to do, and until the end of his service at night (5 sections); (*h,*) of the privileges of fasting, how man is forgiven, and how he is not forgiven (9 sections).

XVII. SUKKAH, OR THE FEAST OF TABERNACLES, in five chapters: (*a* and *b,*) of the size and covering of the Sukkah, how often meals should be eaten in it; exemptions (11 +9 sections) ; (*c* and *d,*) of the palm-branches, myrtle boughs, willows, citrons; what constitutes their fitness, and what not ; how to tie and shake them ; how many days these ceremonies last, of the pouring out of the water (15 + 10 sections); (*c,*) of the rejoicings ; how to divide the offerings and shew-bread on this festival among the orders of the priests (8 sections).

XVIII. YOM TOB, *i.e.*, GOOD DAY, or, as it is generally called BETZAH, *i.e.*, the *egg*, from the word with which it commences, containing 5 chapters; (*a,*) whether an egg laid on the festival day may be eaten thereon. On this question the schools of Shammai and Hillel are divided; the former decide in the affirmative, the latter in the negative (10 sections); (*b,*) of connecting the meals on the Sabbath and other subsequent holy days (9 sections); (*c,*) of catching and killing animals; how to buy the necessary things without mentioning the money (8 sections); (*d,*) of carrying, especially wood not required for burning (7 sections); (*e,*) enumeration and precise definition of classes of things which cannot be done on a feast-day, still less on a Sabbath day (7 sections).

XIX. ROSH HA-SHANAH, OR NEW YEAR, in four chapters: (*a,*) of the four New Years (9 sections); (*b* and *c,*) of examining witnesses who witnessed the new moon, and of announcing it on the top of the mountains by fire, and the New Year with cornets (9 + 8 sections); (*d,*) what to do in case the New Year falls on the Sabbath and of the order of service on the New Year (9 sections).

XX. TAANITH, OR FASTING, in four chapters: (*a,*) of prayer for rain, and proclamation of fasting in case the rain does not come in due season (7 sections): (*b,*) of the ceremonies and prayers on the great fast-days (10 sections); (*c,*) of other occasions of fasting; of not blowing alarms; when to cease fasting, in case it rains (9 sections); (*d,*) of the twenty-four delegates; their fastings, lessons; of bringing wood for the altar (8 sections).

XXI. MEGILLAH, or the ROLL OF THE BOOK OF ESTHER, in four chapters: (*a,*) of the days on which the Megillah is read (11 sections); (*b,*) how to read the Megillah, what can only be done by day, and what can be done by night ; (*c*,) of the sale of holy things ; of the lessons for the Sabbath during the month of Adar, and for other festivals (6 sections) ; (*d*,) of the persons required for the lessons ; of passages to be read or not, etc. (10 sections).

XXII. MOËD KATON, OR SMALL HOLYDAY, in three chapters, treats of the half-holydays between the first and the last day of the Passover, and of the Feast of Tabernacles, and of the work to be done or not (10+5+9 sections).

XXIII. CHAGIGAH, OR FEASTING, in three chapters, speaks of the voluntary sacrifices— other than the paschal lamb—offered by individual Jews on the great feasts, and of sundry ordinances having no direct connection with the subject indicated by the title of the treatise (8+7+8 sections).

III. SEDER NASHIM (WOMEN).

This Seder is composed of seven treatises, viz. :

XXIV. YEBAMOTH enters into the minutest details as to the peculiar Jewish precept of *yibbûm*, or the obligation of marrying the childless widow of a brother, with the alternative disgrace of the performance of the *chalitsah*, or removal of the shoe of the recalcitrant, referred to in the book of Ruth. It contains 16 chapters, in 123 sections. Several portions of this treatise are so offensive to all feelings of delicacy that they have been left untranslated by the English translators.

XXV. KETHUBOTH, in thirteen chapters, contains the laws relating to marriage contracts, to conjugal duties (105 sections).

XXVI. NEDARIM, OR VOWS, in eleven chapters (89 sections).

XXVII. NAZIR, in nine chapters, concerning the Nazarite (60 sections).

XXVIII. SOTAH, or the ERRING WOMAN, in nine chapters and 63 sections. The last sections foretell the signs of the approaching Messiah.

XXIX. GITTIN, OR DIVORCE BILLS, in nine chapters, treats of divorce, and the writing given to the wife, on that occasion ; how it must be written etc. (76 sections).

XXX. KIDDUSHIN, OR BETROTHALS, in four chapters with 47 sections. In the last section we are told that all ass-drivers are wicked, camel-drivers are honest, sailors are pious, physicians are destined for hell, and butchers are company for Amalek.

IV. SEDER NEZIKIN (DAMAGES).

This Seder contains ten tractates.

XXXI. BABA KAMMA, or the FIRST GATE, so called because in the East Law is often administered in the gate-way of a city. It treats, in ten chapters (79 sections), of damages and restitutions.

XXXII. BABA MEZIA, or the MIDDLE GATE, in ten chapters (101 sections), treats of claims resulting from trusts, of buying and selling, etc.

XXXIII. BABA BATHRA or the LAST GATE, treats in ten chapters (90 sections) of the partition of immovables, laws of tenantry, joint occupation, and rights of common, of inheritances, division of property, etc.

XXXIV. SANHEDRIN OR COURTS OF JUSTICE, in eleven chapters (71 sections), treats of the difference of the three tribunals of, a, at least three persons ; b, the small Sanhedrin of 23 persons ; and c, the great Sanhedrin of 71 persons ; of the privileges of the high priest and king; of judges and witnesses of capital punishments.

XXXV. MAKKOTH OR STRIPES, in three chapters (34 sections), treats of corporal punishments.

XXXVI. SHEBUOTH OR OATHS, 8 chapters (62 sections).

XXXVII. EDUYOTH OR TESTIMONIES, 8 chapters (74 sections). It is so called because it consists of laws which tried and trustworthy teachers attested to have been adopted by the elder teachers, in Sanhedrin assembled; at the end we read that Elijah the Prophet will finally determine all disputed points of the sages and will bring peace.

XXXVIII. ABODA ZARAH OR IDOLATRY, 5 chapters (50 sections), treats of the relation between Jews and Gentiles.

XXXIX. ABOTH OR PIRKEY ABOTH, contains in 6 chapters (105 sections), the ethical maxims and sayings of the fathers of the Mishna.

XL. HORAYOTH OR DECISIONS, treats in 3 chapters (20 sections), of the manner of pronouncing sentences and other matters relating to judges and their functions; of prerogatives of the high priest before a common priest, of the learned before the unlearned, etc.

V. SEDER KODASHIM (CONSECRATIONS).

This *Seder* contains eleven tractates.

XLI. ZEBACHIM OR SACRIFICES, treats in 14 chapters (101 sections), of sacrifices, sprinkling of their blood, place of the altar where every sacrifice has to be offered, etc.

XLII. MENACHOTH OR MEAT OFFERINGS, treats in 13 chapters (93 sections), of meat offerings, and things pertaining to them.

XLIII. CHULLIN OR UNCONSECRATED

THINGS are treated in 12 chapters (74 sections), together with other things, as what animals are unlawful, or the pollution communicated by an unlawful animal, etc.

XLIV. BECHOROTH OR FIRST-BORN, treats in 9 chapters (73 sections), of the first-born and the precepts and rights concerningly.

XLV. ERACHIN OR ESTIMATES, treats in 9 chapters (49 sections), of the person who has to make the estimate and on what and how.

XLVI. TEMURAH OR EXCHANGES, in 7 chapters (35 sections), treats of the way exchanges are to be offered between sacred things.

XLVII. KERITHUTH OR CUTTING OFF, in 7 chapters (43 sections), treats of offenders being cut off from the Lord, provided the offences were wantonly committed: but if inadvertently committed, entail the obligation to bring sin offerings.

XLVIII. MEÏLA OR TRESPASS, treats of things partaking of the name of the sacrilege 6 chapters (38 sections).

XLIX. TAMID OR DAILY SACRIFICES, in 7 chapters (34 sections), treats of the morning and evening offerings and the work connected with them.

L. MIDDOTH OR MEASUREMENTS, in 5 chapters (34 sections), treats of the measurements of the Temple, its different parts and courts.

LI. KINNIM OR BIRDS' NESTS, treats in 3 chapters (15 sections), of the mistakes about doves and beasts brought into the Temple for sacrifice.

VI. SEDER TOHAROTH (PURIFICATIONS).

This order has twelve tractates.

LII. KELIM OR VESSELS, in 30 chapters

(254 sections), treats of those which convey uncleanness.

LIII. OHALOTH OR TENTS, in 18 chapters, (134 sections), treats of tents and houses retaining uncleanness, etc.

LIV. NEGAÏM OR PLAGUES OF LEPROSY, in 14 chapters (115 sections), treats of leprosy of men, garments or dwellings.

LV. PARAH OR THE RED HEIFER, in 12 chapters (95 sections), directs how she is to be burned, of her age, and what may make her unfit, etc.

LVI. TOHAROTH OR PURIFICATIONS, in 10 chapters (92 sections), teaches how purifications are to be effected.

LVII. MIKVAOTH OR POOLS OF WATER, in 10 chapters (71 sections), treats of the *mikvâh* or bathing place, its construction, and the quantity of water necessary for cleansing ; or when a mikvah becomes unfit for bathing, etc.

LVIII. NIDDAH OR SEPARATION of women during their menses, after childbirth, etc., 10 chapters (79 sections).

LIX. MACHSHIRIN OR LIQUORS that dispose seeds and fruits to receive pollution, 6 chapters (54 sections).

LX. ZABIM OR BODILY FLUXES that cause pollution, 5 chapters (32 sections).

LXI. TEBUL YOM OR BAPTISM ON THE DAY OF UNCLEANNESS, 4 chapters (26 sections).

LXII. YADAÏM OR HANDS, 4 chapters (21 sections), treats of the washing of hands and of the disputes between the Pharisees and Sadducees concerningly, of the canonicity of certain parts in and of certain books of the Old Testament.

LXIII. UKZIN OR STALKS OF FRUIT which convey uncleanness, in 3 chapters (28 sections).

EDITIONS OF THE MISHNA.

The Mishna has been often published. The first edition was published at Naples, 1492, with the commentary of Maimonides. With the same commentary and that of Obadiah di Bertinoro, it was published at Riva di Trento, 1559, and Venice, 1606. The text alone with vowel-points was published at Amsterdam, 1646; in the latter place was also published, 1698-1703, the splendid edition of Surenhusius, giving besides the text in the original and Latin, also the commentaries of Maimonides and Obadiah di Bertinoro in Latin, notes, etc., 6 vols. folio. An edition, giving the text with vowels and a German translation in Hebrew letters, was published, Berlin, 1832-'34, 6 vols. Of recent editions we mention the Mishna with the Commentary of Bertinoro and a Judaco-German translation in Hebrew letters, published at Warsaw, 1882, 6 vols.; an edition containing besides the Commentaries of Bertinoro and Heller, twelve other commentaries, was published at Wilna, 1886, 6 vols. Of late the Mishna has been published from a MS. preserved at Cambridge, under the title : *The Mishnah, on which the Palestinian Talmud rests*, edited by W. H. Lowe, Cambridge, 1883.

TRANSLATIONS OF THE MISHNAH.

Besides the Latin version of Surenhuys, several treatises have also been translated into Latin by different authors, which we pass over. Into *Spanish* it was translated by Abraham ben Reuben, Venice, 1606; into *German* by Rabe, Ausbach, 1760-'63, 6 parts, and Josh, Berlin, 1832-'33, 6 vols. (the trans-

5

lation is in Rabbinic letters.) We have not
as yet a complete *English* translation, but this
want the present writer hopes to supply. Of
the several treatises, the following are translated in the collections of De Sola and Raph-
ael (London, 1845), and of Barclay (1878).
1. *Berachoth* (De Sola, Barclay), 2. *Kilayim* (De Sola), 3. *Shebüth* (Barclay), 4.
Shabbath (De Sola, Barclay, but the latter
has only translated one-third. The remaining two-thirds, he says, are devoid of interest,
and in parts unfit for publication.) 5. *Erubin* (De Sola), 6. *Pesachim*, 7. *Yoma*, 8.
Sukkah (both), 9. *Beza* (De Sola), 10.
Rosh-hashana, 11. *Taanith* (both), 12.
Megillah, 13. *Moëd Katon* (De Sola), 14.
Chagiga (Barclay), 15. *Jebamoth* (De Sola.
Besides chapters vi. and vii. several sections were omitted by the translators, the
contents, as they state, not being suited
to the refined notions of the English
readers.) 16. *Kethuboth*, 17. *Gittin*, 18.
Kiddushin (De Sola), 19. *Sanhedrin*, 20.
Aboda Sara, 21. *Aboth* (Barclay), 22.
Chullin (De Sola), 23. *Tamid*, 24. *Mid-
doth*, 25. *Negaïm*, 26. *Para* (Barclay),
27. *Jadayim* (both). No treatise has so often
been translated as the treatise *Aboth.* The
best English edition is that by Taylor,
Sayings of the Fathers (Cambridge, 1877).
The Treatise *Middoth* has also been translated by Edersheim, and is found in his
Sketches of Jewish Social Life, p. 297, *seq.*,
London.

INTRODUCTION TO THE MISHNA.

Of works especially devoted to the Mishna,
we mention Frankel (*Hodegetica*, Leipsic,
1859), Brüll (*Einleitung*, Frankfort, 1876), and
Weiss (*Zur Geschichte der Jüdischen Tradi-*

tion, vols. I and II, Vienna, 1871, 1877), but all these works are written in Hebrew.

PHILOLOGICAL HELPS.

Hartmann, *Thesauri linguæ Hebraicæ e Mischna augendi particula* I, II, III, Rostock 1825-'26. Dukes, *Die Sprache der Mischna lexicographisch und grammatisch betrachtet,* Esslingen, 1846. Weiss, *Studien über die Sprache der Mischna,* Vienna, 1867 (Hebrew). Geiger, *Lehr und Lesebuch zur Sprache der Mischnah,* Breslau, 1845 (2 parts).

R. Juda's Mishna, however, did not contain all expositions. Many others existed which are contained in part in the *Sifre* on Leviticus, *Sifri* on Numbers and Deuteronomy, *Mechilta* on Exodus, the Mishnas made by individual teachers for the use of their pupils, with the addition of the official Mishna collected by R. Chiya and his cotemporaries. All the Halakhoth of this sort, which were extra-Mishnaic, were called *Baraithoth,* also *Toseftoth.* Juda, it is true, collected the great mass of traditions in the work called Mishna; "but even this copious work could not satisfy, for the length of time, the zeal of the rabbins for the law, for all casuistry is endless in its details. There were a great multitude of all kinds of possibilities which were treated in the Mishna, and yet, again, each single sentence left open divers possibilities, divers doubts, and considerations not yet finished. Thus it was an inner necessity of the matter that the text of the Mishna should again become the point of learned discussion. Partly by means of logic (that is, Rabbinical), partly with the help of the traditional matter, which had not yet been included in the Mishna, all open questions were now discussed. This task was carried

out by the Amoraïm, or Gemarical doctors,
whose very *singular* illustrations, opinions,
and doctrines were subsequently to form the
Gemaras, *i. e.* the Palestinian and Babylonian:
a body of men charged with being the most
learned and elaborate triflers that ever
brought discredit upon the republic of letters :—

> " For mystic learning, wondrous able,
> In magic, talisman, and cabal—
> Deep-sighted in intelligences,
> Ideas, atoms, influences. "—

With unexampled assiduity did they seek
after or invent obscurities and ambiguities,
which continually furnished pretexts for new
expositions and illustrations, the art of cloud-
ing texts in themselves clear having proved
ever less difficult than that of elucidating
passages the words or the sense of which might
be really involved in obscurity.

> " Hence comment after comment, spun as fine
> As bloated spiders draw the flimsy line."

The two main schools where this casuistic
treatment of the Mishnic text was exercised
were that at Tiberias, in Palestine, and that
at Sora, in Babylonia, whither Abba Areka,
called Rab, a pupil of R. Juda, had brought
the Mishna. In these and other schools (as
Nahardea, Sipporis, Pumbaditha and Jabne)
the thread of casuistry was twisted over and
over again ; and the matter of traditions of
the law thus took greater and greater dimensions. Abandoning the scripture text, to
illustrate and to explain which the doctors
and wise men of the schools had hitherto labored, successive generations of *Gemarici* now
devoted their whole attention to the exposition of the text of the Mishna ; and the industry and cavillation were such that expositions, illustrations and commentaries multi-

plied with amaziug rapidity and to so por-
tentous a degree that they eventually swelled
into a monstrous chaotic mass, which was dig-
nified by the name of *Gemara*, *i. e.*, "Supplement" or "Complement," and this, together
with the Mishna, was called "Talmud,"

Notwithstanding the uncertain paternity
of this incongruous body of opinions, there
were not wanting those who gave a prefer-
ence to the Gemara over the Mishna, and
even over the "written law." It was said by
some that the "written law" was like water,
the Mishna like wine, and the Gemara like
hippocras, or spiced wine. The "words of
the scribes," said those supporters of the Gemara are lovely above the "words of the law,"
for the "words of the law" are *weighty and
light*, but the "words of the scribes," are all
"weighty."[1]   It was by R. Jochanan ben Eliezer, called also *Bar Naphha* or the "Son of
the Blacksmith," rector of the academy of
Tiberias, that the minor chaos of comment
and facetiæ began to be collected about A.D
260, and these, being added to the Mishna
were termed the *Palestinian Talmud*, or *Talmud Jerushalmi*, *i. e.*, "Jerusalem Talmud."

THE JERUSALEM TALMUD.

This important commentary on the
Mishna, which was completed about A.D.
350, has not come down to us entire; what
we have at this day in our own hands is only
on the four orders *Zeraim*, *Moëd*, *Nashim*
Nezikim, and the first three chapters of the
treatise *Niddah* (in the sixth order). But
the Jerusalem Talmud has a Gemara on the
entire first order, whereas the Babylonian has
it only on the first treatise of that order, and

---

1. Comp. my art. "Talmud" in *McClintock and Strong's Cy-
clopædia*.

70   *THE TALMUD;*

a Gemara to the treatise *Shekalim*, which is also wanting in the Babylonian Talmud.

The language of the Jerusalem Talmud is Talmudic Hebrew, with a strong infusion of the Western Aramaic, then common in Palestine. The general contents of the Gemara may be classified into *Halakhoth* and *Haggadoth;* principles or rules of jurisprudence and legendary illustrations. The Haggadoth were often published. A German translation was published by A. Wünshe, Zurich, 1880.

The Jerusalem Talmud was first published by D. Bomberg at Venice, without date ; then with brief glosses at Cracow in 1609, and Krotoschin, 1866, folio; an edition in 4 vols. was published at Shitomir, 1860-1867. A Latin translation of the greater part of the Jerusalem Gemara is found in Ugolino's *Thesaurus Antiqq. Sacr.;* viz. vol. xvii.: *Pesachim ;* vol. xviii.: *Shekalim, Yoma, Sukka, Roshhashana, Taanith, Megilla, Hagiga, Beza, Moëd Katon ;* vol. xx.: *Maaseroth, Challa, Orla, Bikkurim ;* vol. xxv.: *Sanhedrin, Maccoth ;* vol. xxx. : *Kiddushin, Sota, Kethuboth.* The first treatise, *Berachoth,* of the Jerusalem and Babylonian Gemara was translated into German by Rabe, Halle, 1777; the same matter was translated into French by Chiarini, Leipsic, 1831. A French translation of the entire Jerusalem Talmud was undertaken by M. Schwab. The first volume was published at Paris, 1872, the ninth, in 1887. Two more volumes will complete the entire work. The best work on the Jerusalem Talmud is the *Introduction* published by Z. Frankel, Breslau, 1870 (Hebrew).

From the schools of Babylonia, also, a similar collection was in after-times made, but, as upon the desolation of Palestine, the study of the law was chiefly prosecuted in Babylon, the colleges there were far more numerous, and far more ingenious and prolific were the imaginations of the Babylonian professors. To collect and methodize all the disputations, interpretations, elucidations, commentaries, and conceits of the Babylonian Gemarici was consequently a labor neither of one man nor of a single age. The first attempt was made (A.D. 367) by R. Ashe ben Simai, surnamed Rabban, *i. e.*, our teacher, elected at the age of fourteen to be rector of the school of Sora. At the outset of his administration, Ashe found the immense mass of Gemara learning in a chaotic confusion. The text of the Mishna itself had become deteriorated by various readings, and the current explanations of many points in it were uncertain and contradictory. One master had laid down this, and another that; and the details of practice in Jewish life were thereby growing more and more irregular. The Jerusalem Talmud was imperfect as a commentary on the Mishna, both as to the extent and the quality of its qualifications. Many parts of the text were left without Gemara, and the commentary on those parts, professedly explained, was weakened and often worthless by a large admixture of mere fable and legend. Under these circumstances Ashe was moved to undertake a connected and comprehensive commentary on the treatises of the Mishna, so as to collect, condense, and set in order the entire array of traditional law, as eliminated by the rabbins since the time of Juda the Great. This was the enterprise of his life, and one which, after the lapse of many laborious years, resulted in the consolidation of the *Babylonian Talmud*.

Ashe, who died in 427, only had arranged thirty-five books, but the work inaugurated by him, was progressively advanced by his successors, till its completion and sealing in

the year 498 by Rabbi Abina, with whom
ended the series and succession of the
Amoraïm, or Mishna and Talmud authorities
at Sora. "Denominated, from the name of
the province in which it was first compiled,
the *Babylonian Talmud*, this second Talmud
is as unmanageable to the student on account
of its style and composition as on account of
its prodigious bulk. Composed in a dialect
neither Chaldaic nor Hebrew, but a barbarous
commixture of both of these and of other dia-
lects, jumbled together in defiance of all the
rules of composition or of grammar, it affords a
second specimen of a Babylonian *confusion of
languages*.

> " It was a parti-colored dress
>   Of patched and piebald languages,
>   Which made some think, when it did gabble.
>   They'd heard three laborers of Babel,
>   Or Cerberus himself pronounce
>   A leash of languages at once."

Abounding, moreover, in fantastic trifles
and Rabbinical reveries, it must appear
almost incredible that any sane man could
exhibit such acumen and such ardor in the
invention of those unintelligible comments, in
those nice scrupulosities, and those ludicrous
chimeras which the rabbins have solemnly
published to the world, and of which we will
speak further on.[1]

THE TALMUD.

The Talmud (from *lamad* " to teach") is next
to (or rather, in the strictly Jewish view,
along with) the canonical Scriptures, the
authoritative code of Hebrew doctrine and
jurisprudence.[2]   It consists of the Mishna

---

[1] Comp. my art. *l. c.*
[2] The Jews divided their law into the written and unwritten. The
latter, which is also called " the oral law," it is claimed to have
been delivered to Joshua by Moses, who again received it on

as text, and a voluminous collection of commentaries and illustrations, called in the more modern Hebrew, *horaa*, and in Aramaic *Gemara*, "the complement," or "completion" from *gamar*, to make perfect. The men therefore who delivered these decisive commentaries are called *gemarists*, sometimes *horaïm*, but more commonly *Amoraïm*.

In general the Gemara takes the character of scholastic discussions, more or less prolonged, on the consecutive portions of the Mishna.[1] On a cursory view, it is true, these discussions have the air of a desultory and confused wrangle, but when studied more carefully, they resolve themselves into a system governed by a methodology of its

---

Mount Sinai. Appeal is therefore often made to these so called "precepts delivered to Moses on Mount Sinai," and the more so because these "precepts" belong to the class of undisputed decisions.

1. As an example we quote the following from the very first page of the Talmud : *Mishna*—" At what time in the evening should one say the Shema ? * From the time that the priests go in to eat of their oblation till the end of the first night-watch. These are the words of Rabbi Eliezer, but the wise men say until midnight. Rabban Gamaliel says till the morning dawn ariseth. It came to pass that his sons were returning from a banquet ; they said unto him, ' We have not yet recited the Shema.' He answered and said unto them, ' If the morning dawn has not yet arisen, ye are under obligation to recite it.' And not this alone have they said, but everywhere where the wise have said ' until midnight,' the command is binding till the morning dawn ariseth ; and the burning of the fat and of the joints is lawful until the morning dawn ariseth, and so everything which may be eaten on the same day is allowed to be eaten till the rise of the morning dawn. If so, why do the sages say ' till midnight ? ' In order to keep a man far from transgressing.—*Gemara*. The Tanna (*i.e.*, the author of the Mishna), what is his authority that he teaches, from what time onward ? And, besides that, why does he teach on the evening first, and might he teach on the morning first ? The Tanna rests on the Scripture, for it is written, ' When thou liest down and when thou risest up,' and so he teaches the time of reciting the Shema, when thou liest down, when is it ? From the time when the priests go in to eat of their oblation. But if thou wilt, say I, he hath taken it out of the creation of the world, for it is said, it was evening, and it was morning one day. If this is so, why does a later Mishna teach that at dawn two benedictions are to be said before the Shema, and one after ; and in the evening two before and two after ; and yet they teach in the evening first. The Tanna begins in the evening, then he teaches in the morning ; as he treats of the morning so he explains the things of the morning, and then he explains the things of the evening."—This is less than one-fourth part of the comment in the Gemara, on that passage in the Mishna, and the rest is equally lucid and interesting.

* The well-known prayer, beginning " Hear, O Israel."

own. [1]   The language of the Talmud is partly Hebrew and partly Aramaic. The best Hebrew of the work is in the text of the Mishna, that in the Gemara being largely debased with exotic words of various tongues, barbarous spelling, and uncouth grammatical or rather ungrammatical forms. The same remark will apply to the Aramaic portions, which in general are those containing popular narrative or legendary illustration, while the law principles, and the discussions relating to them, are embodied in Hebrew. Many forms of the Talmudic dialect, are so peculiar as to render a grammar adapted to the work itself greatly to be desired. Ordinary Hebrew grammar will not take a man through a page of it.

In style the Mishna is remarkable for its extreme conciseness, [2] and the Gemara is written upon the same model, though not so frequently obscure. The prevailing principle of the composition seems to have been the employment of the fewest words, thus rendering the work a constant brachylogy. A phrase becomes the focus of many thoughts ; a solitary word, an anagram, a cipher for a whole subject of reflection. To employ an appropriate expression of Delitzsch [3] : " What Jean Paul says of the style

---

1. "Non vero sterilis in Mishnicam commentarius Gemara est ; quae filius tantum modo verba explicet. Sed *prolixas in eam instituit disputationes*, quaestiones proponendo et ad eos respondendo, dubia movendo, eaque solvendo, excipiendo et replicando," Waehner *Antiqq. Hebr.* 1, p. 339.

2. Waehner. *l. c.* p.241 : "Nostro quidem judicio vix quicquam est, quod in bene scripto libro laudari possit, exquo Mishnicum hoc opus commentari non mereatur. Dictio pura hebraica est, quae concisa brevi'ate, pro istorum temporum more, res propemodum infinitas proponit. Quae quidem brevitas in causa est, ut a rerum Judaicarum et istorum temporum styli rudibus hoc liber non intelligatur. Sed imperitis non scripsit R. Juda sanctus, sed viris eruditis, quos haec brevitas mirum in modum delectat. Si qua alicubi esse videatur *obscuritas*, evanescet, dummodo orationis genus sibi familiare red iere lector laboret. ·Tam *accurate et cogitate cuncta* scripsit, quamqui accuratissime. Vix ullo vel *excessu* vel *defectu* liber laborat," etc.

3. *Zur Geschichte der Jüdischen Poesie*, p. 31.

of Haman, applies exactly to that of the Talmud: it is a firmament of telescopic stars, containing many a cluster of light which no unaided eye has ever resolved."

But without regard to grammatical and linguistic difficulties and numberless abbreviations which crowd the pages of the Talmud, there are a number of *termini technici*, which were current only in the rabbinical schools, but have been incorporated in the Gemara like joints and ligaments in its organization, so as to make the knowledge of them indispensable to the student.

Since the Gemara is in general only a more complete development of the Mishna, it follows the same routine of the six orders of the latter, and besides the primary elements of the Mishna, as quotations from Scripture, rules and regulations, ordinances, prescribed customs and rites, the text of the Mishna is yet enlarged by innumerable fragments of *Toseftoth* or appendices to the Mishna, and *Boraïthoth* or supplements to the Mishna, as the books *Sifra, Sifri and Mechi'ta*, inserted here and there throughout the entire frame of the work. Besides these materials there are an endless variety of *Haggadoth*, anecdotes and illustrations, historical and legendary, poetical allegories, charming parables, witty epithalamiums, etc., the understanding of which taxes the ingenuity and patience of the Christian student, and we can well appreciate words of the learned Dr. Lightfoot, when he thus complains of the authors of the Talmud: "The almost unconquerable difficulty of their style, the frightful roughness of their language, and the amazing emptiness and sophistry of the matters handled, do torture, vex, and tire him that reads them. They do everywhere abound with trifles in that man-

ner as though they had no mind to be read ;
with obscurities and difficulties as though
they had no mind to be understood ; so that
the reader hath need of patience all along to
enable him to bear both trifling in sense and
roughness in expression."

Besides the materials mentioned already,
there are subsidiaries to the Talmud, printed
either in the margin of the pages or at the
end of the treatises, viz. 1. the *Tosaphoth*, exegetical additions by later authors—which
must not be confounded with the *Toseftoth ;*
2, *Masorah ha-shesh Sedarim*, being marginal
Masoretic indexes to the six orders of the
Mishna ; 3, *Aïn* or *En-Mishpat, i. e.*, index of
places on the rites and institutions : 4, *Ner
Mitsvoth*, a general index of decisions according to the digest of Maimonides ; and 5, *Per-
ushim*, or commentaries by different authors.

Besides the 63 treatises which compose the
Mishna and Gemara, there are certain minor
ones which are connected with the Talmud
as a kind of Apocrypha or appendix, under
the title of *Mesiktoth K'tanoth* or smaller treatises. These are :

1. *Sopherim*, concerning the scribe and
reader of the law (21 chapters). This treatise
is important for the Masorah. A separate
edition with notes, was published by J. Mül-
ler (Leipsic, 1878).

2. *Kallah*, relates to marriages (1 chapter).

3. *Ebel Rabbathi*, or *Semachoth*, concerning
the ordinances for funeral solemnities (14
chapters).

4. *Derck Erets*, on social duties (11 chapters).

5. *Derck Erets Sutta*, rules for the learned
(10 chapters).

6. *Perck ha-Shalom*, on the love of peace
(1 chapter).

7. *Gerim*, concerning proselytes (4 chapters). *

8. *Kuthim*, concerning Samaritans (2 chapters). *

9. *Abadim*, concerning slaves (3 chapters).*

10. *Tsitsith*, concerning fringes (1 chapter). *

11. *Tephillin*, concerning phylacteries (1 chapter). *

12. *Mezuzah*, concerning the writing on the door-post (2 chapters). *

13. *Sepher Thorah*, concerning the writing of the law (5 chapters). *

14. *Hilcoth Erets Israel*, relating to the ways of slaughtering animals for food after the Jewish ideas, a treatise which is much later than the Talmud.

15. *Aboth di-Rabbi Nathan*, a commentary on or amplification of the treatise (21 chapters), recently published with notes, etc., by S. Schechter, Vienna, 1887.

In order to enable the student to find at once in which of the twelve volumes of the Babylonian Talmud the different treatises of the Mishna are treated, we subjoin the following table, giving in the first column the names of the treatises in alphabetical order; in the second the volume of the Talmud; in the third the *Seder* or order, under which they are given, and in the fourth the numerical order in which they stand in the Mishna.

(SEE TABLE, PAGE 78.)

LITERARY AND MORAL CHARACTER OF THE BOOK.

Buxtorf, the famous scholar in Rabbinic lore, characterizes the Talmud as follows: " Sunt enim in Talmude adhuc multa quoque

---

* Published also separately by R. Kirchheim under the title *Septem Libri Talmudici Parvi*, Frankfort, 1851.

Name.	Vol.	Order.
Aboth	IX	Nezikin
Aboda Zarah	VIII	"
Baba Bathra	VII	"
" Kamma		"
" Mezia		"
Bechoroth	X	Kodashim
Bera-choth	I	Zeraim
Beza	III	Moëd
Bikkurim	I	Zeraim
Chagiga	III	Moëd
Challah	I	Zeraim
Chullin	XI	Kodashim
Demai	I	Zeraim
Eduyoth	IX	Nezikin
Erachin	XI	Kodashim
Erubin	III	Moëd
Gittin	VI	Nashim
Horajoth	IX	Nezikin
Kelim	XII	Tohoroth
Keritbuth	XI	Kodashim
Kethuboth	V	Nashim
Kiddushin		"
Kilajim	I	Zeraim
Kinnim	XI	Kodashim
Maascroth	I	Zeraim
Maaser sheni		"
Makkoth	IX	Nezikin
Machshirin	XII	Tohoroth
Megillah	IV	Moëd
Meila	XI	Kodashim
Middoth		"
Mikwaoth	XII	Tohoroth

Name.	Vol.	Order.	Trea-tise.
Menachoth	X	Kodashim	3
Moëd Katon	III	Moëd	11
Nazir	VI	Nashim	6
Nedarim	"	"	5
Negaim	XII	Tohoroth	3
Nidda	"	"	7
Ohaloth	"	"	2
Orla	I	Zeraim	10
Parah	XII	Tohoroth	4
Peah	I	Zeraim	2
Pesachim	III	Moëd	8
Rosh-hashana	IV	"	4
Sanhedrim	IX	Nezikin	1
Shabbath	II	Moëd	5
Shekalim	IV	"	6
Sheblith	I	Zeraim	7
Shebuoth	IX	Nezikin	6
Sotah	VI	Nashim	0
Sukka	IV	Moëd	9
Taanith	"	"	6
Tamid	XI	Kodashim	0
Tebul yom	XII	Tohoroth	9
Temura	XI	Kodashim	6
Terumoth	I	Zeraim	6
Tohoroth	XII	Tohoroth	5
Ukzin	"	"	
Yadaim	"	"	
Yebamoth	V	Nashim	5
Yoma	IV	Moëd	9
Zabim	XII	Tohoroth	7
Zebachim	X	Kodashim	6

Theologica sana, quamvis plurimis inutilibus corticibus, ut Majemon alicubi loquitur, involuta. Sunt in eo multa fida antiquitatis Judaicae collapsae veluti rudera et vestigia, ad convincendam posterorum Judaeorum perfidiam, ad illustrandam utriusque testamenti historiam, ad recte explicandos ritus, leges, consuetudines populi Hebraei prisci, plurimum conducentia. Sunt in eo multa Juridica, Medica, Physica, Ethica, Politica, Astronomica et aliarum scientiarum praeclara documenta, quae istius gentis et temporis historiam mirifice commendant," etc. [1] According to Buxtorf, the Talmud contains all and everything, and this we will illustrate by the following examples:

1. God. "The day," we are told, "contains twelve hours. The first three hours, the Holy One, blessed be He, sits and studies the law. The second three hours, He sits and judges the whole world. The third three hours He sits and feeds all the world, from the horns of the unicorns to the eggs of the vermin. In the fourth three hours He sits and plays with leviathan, for it is said (Ps. civ., 26) 'The Leviathan whom thou hast formed to play therewith.' "—*Aboda Zarah* (fol. 3, col. 2).

Rabbi Eliezer says, "The night has three watches, and at every watch, the Holy One, blessed be He, sits and roars like a lion, for it is said, 'The Lord shall roar from on high, and utter his voice from his holy habitation: roaring he shall roar upon his habitation.'" (Jer. xxv., 30). *Berachoth* fol. 3, col. 1.

Rabbi Isaac, the son of Samuel, says, in the name of Rav, "The night has three watches, and at every watch, the Holy One, blessed be He, sits and roars like a lion, and says, 'Woe is me that I have laid desolate my house, and burned my sanctuary, and sent my children into captivity amongst the nations of the earth.'" (*Ibid.*).

God is presented as praying (*l. c.* fol. 7, col. 1), and wearing phylacteries (*ibid.*). When He weeps on account of his children. He lets two tears fall into the Great Ocean, the noise of which is heard from one end of the world to the other, and this is an earthquake (*l. c.* fol. 59, col. 1). It is further said that He "braided the hair of Eve" (*l. c.* fol. 61, col. 1), and "shaved the head of Sennacherib." (*Sanhedrin* fol. 96, col. 1).

These are only a very few items of the very many examples

---

1. Preface to his *Lexicon Chald. et Talmud.*

which could be adduced concerning the Deity. That these stories are extravagant, and often, when taken literally, absurd, no one can deny. But they must be merely regarded as to their meaning and intention. Much has been said against the Talmud on account of the preposterous character of some of these stories. But we should give the Hebrew *literati* the benefit of their own explanations. They tell us that in the Talmud the Haggadah has no absolute authority, nor any value except in the way of elucidation. It often—but not always—enwraps a philosophic meaning under the veil of allegory, mythic folk-lore, ethical story, oriental romance, parable, and aphorism and fable. They deny that the authors of these fancy pieces intended either to add to the law of God or to detract from it by them, but only to explain and enforce it in terms best suited to the popular capacity. They caution us against receiving these things according to the letter, and admonish us to understand them according to their spiritual or moral import. " Beware," says Maimonides, " that you take not the words of the wise men literally, for this would be degrading to the sacred doctrine, and sometimes contradict it. Seek rather the hidden sense, and if you cannot find the kernel, let the shell alone, and confess,' I cannot understand this.'" But the impartial reader must at once admit that these suggestions are merely the after-thoughts of tender apologists, for some of these stories, as we shall see further on, have no hidden sense at all, but must be taken literally, because meant so.

2. ASTROLOGY. It is surprising that men who believe in a divine revelation, should have so much to say about things which savor of heathenism, and treat astrology as a science which governs the life of man. Thus we are told : " The stars make men wise, the stars make men rich." (*Shabbath* fol. 156, col. 1). " A man born on the first day of the week will excel in only one quality. He that is born on the second day will be an angry man, because on that day the waters were divided. He that is born on the third day of the week will be rich and licentious, because on it the herbs were created. He that is born on the fourth day will be wise and of good memory, because on that day the lights were hung up. He that is born on the fifth day will be charitable, because on that day the fishes and fowls were created. He that is born on the Sabbath, on the Sabbath he shall also die, because on his account they profaned the great Sabbath day." Rabba bar Shila says : "He shall be eminently holy." (*ibid*). Rabbi Hanina says : " The influence of the stars makes wise, the influence of the stars makes rich, and Israel is under the influence of the stars." Rabbi Jochanan says : " Israel is not under the influence of the stars. Whence is it proved ? ' Thus saith the Lord, Learn not the way of the heathen, and be not dismayed at the signs of heaven, for the heathen are dismayed at them.' (Jer. x., 2). The heathen, but not Israel" (*ibid.*). Astrology naturally leads to amulets and charms.

3. AMULETS. Amulets are divided into two classes, ap-

proved and disapproved. "What is an approved amulet?" Any amulet that has effected a cure, and done so twice or thrice," (*ibid.* fol. 61, col. 1).

4. CHARMS. "For the bleeding of the nose, let a man be brought who is a priest, and whose name is Levi, and let him write the word Levi backwards. If this cannot be done, get a layman, and let him write the following words backwards: 'Ana pipi Shila bar Sumki;' or let him write these words: 'Taam dli bemi Keseph, taam li bemi paggan.' Or let him take a root of grass, and the cord of an old bed, and paper and saffron and the red part of the inside of a palm-tree, and let him burn them together, and let him take some wool and twist two threads, and let him dip them in vinegar, and then roll them in the ashes and put them into his nose. Or let him look out for a small stream of water that flows from east to west, and let him go and stand with one leg on each side of it, and let him take with his right hand some mud from under his left foot, and with his left hand from under his right foot, and let him twist two threads of wool, and dip them in the mud, and put them into his nostrils. Or let him be placed under a spout, and let water be brought and poured upon him, and let them say, 'As this water ceases to flow, so let the blood of M, the son of M, also cease.'" (*Gittin* fol. 69, col. 1). A commentary on this wisdom or folly is superfluous. That this direction to stop a bleeding at the nose is not a rare case in the Talmud, the following mode of treatment for the bite of a mad dog will prove. If a man be bitten by a mad dog he must die; what, then, is the remedy? "Abaï says he must take the skin of a male adder and write upon it these words: 'I, M. the son of the woman N, upon the skin of a male adder, write against thee, Kanti Kanti Klirus, but some say, Kandi Kandi Klurus, Lord of Hosts, Amen. Selah!' Let him also cast off his clothes and bury them in a graveyard for twelve months of a year; then let him take them up, and burn them in a furnace, and let him strew the ashes at the parting of the roads, and during these twelve months let him only drink out of a brass tube, lest he see the phantom form of the demon, and he be endangered. This was done by Abba, the son of Martha, who is the same as Abba, the son of Maujumi. His mother made a golden tube for him." (*Yoma* fol. 83, col. 1).

DEMONS. Abba Benjamin says, "If leave had been given to see the hurtful demons, no creature could stand before them." Abbai says, "They are more than we are, and stand against us, like the trench round a garden bed." Rav Huna says, "Everyone has a thousand on his left hand, and ten thousand on his right hand." Rabba says, "The want of room at the sermon is from them, the wearing out of the Rabbi's clothes is from their rubbing against them, bruised legs are from them." "Whosoever wishes to know their existence, let him take ashes passed through a sieve, and strew them in his bed, and in the morning he will see the marks of a cock's claws. Whosoever wishes

6

to see them let him take the interior covering of a black-cat,
the kitten of a first-born black cat, which is also the kitten of
a first-born, and let him burn it in the fire, and powder it,
and fill his eyes with it, and he will see them. But let him
pour the powder into an iron tube, and seal it with an iron
signet, lest they should steal any of it, and let him also seal
up the mouth thereof, lest any harm ensue. Rav Bibi bar
Abbai did thus, and he was harmed, but the rabbis prayed
for mercy, and he was healed." (*Berachoth* fol. 6, col. 1.)

We could fill pages by reciting pretty stories about
Adam, Solomon, the worm shamir, the fabulous river
Sambation, Lilith, Titus, Leviathan, etc., but *sapienti sat.*

In the face of such extravagancies, we are not surprised
at the following statement made by a modern Jewish writer,
the late H. Hurwitz, in an essay preceding his *Hebrew
Tales* (London, 1826), p. 34 sq.:

"The Talmud contains many things which every enlightened Jew must sincerely wish had either never appeared
there, or should, at least, long ago have been expunged
from its pages. Some of these stories are objectionable
per se., others are, indeed, susceptible of explanations, but
without them are calculated to produce false and erroneous
impressions.

" Of the former description are all those extravagancies relating to the extent of Paradise, the dimensions of Gehi-
nom, the size of Leviathan, and the *Shor Habar*, the freaks
of *Ashmadai*, etc., etc.,—idle tales, borrowed most probably
from the Parthians and Arabians, to whom the Jews were
subject before the promulgation of the Talmud. These
absurdities are as foreign to genuine religion as they are
repugnant to common sense.

"How those objectionable passages came at
all to be inserted, can only be accounted for
from that great reverence with which the
Israelites of those days used to regard their
wise men · and which made them look upon
every word and expression that dropped
from the mouth of their instructors as so
many precious sayings, well worthy of being
preserved. These they wrote down for their
own private information, together with more
important matters. And when, in after-
times, those writings were collected, in order
to be embodied in one entire work, the col-
lectors, either from want of proper discrimi-
nation, or from some pious motive, suffered
them to remain ; and thus they were handed
down to posterity. That the wiser portion

of the nation never approved of them is well known. Nay, that some of the Talmudists themselves regard them with no very favorable eye, is plain, from the bitter terms in which they exclaimed against them.

" I admit also that there are many and various contradictions in the Talmud, and, indeed, it would be a miracle were there none. For let it be recollected that this work contains, not the opinions of only a few individuals living in the same society, under precisely similar circumstances, but of hundreds, nay, I might without exaggeration say, of thousands of learned men, of various talents, living in a long series of ages, in different countries, and under the most diversified conditions.

" To believe that its multifarious contents are all dictates of unerring wisdom, is as extravagant as to suppose that all it contains is founded in error. Like all other productions of unaided humanity, it is not free from mistakes and prejudices, to remind us that the writers were fallible men, and that unqualified admiration must be reserved for the works of divine inspiration, which we ought to study, the better to adore and obey the all-perfect Author. But while I should be among the first to protest against any confusion of the Talmudic Rills with the ever-flowing Stream of Holy Writ, I do not hesitate to avow my doubts, whether there exists any uninspired work of equal antiquity, that contains more interesting, more various, and valuable information than that of the still existing remains of the ancient Hebrew Sages."

But while we admire the candor of this Jewish writer, we must confess that not all of his co-religionists act on the same principle, as the sequel will prove. Forty years after Mr. Hurwitz had published his *Hebrew Tales*, an article appeared in the *Quarterly Review* for October, 1867, with the heading "What is the Talmud?" Such a panegyric the Talmud most likely never had. Superficial as this article was,[1] yet its brilliant style created quite a sensation, and the more so because it contained sentences which could not have emanated from a Jew. But the writer was a Jew, the late E. Deutsch, and what Isaac said to Jacob, "The voice is Jacob's voice, but the hands are the hands of Esau," must be applied to the author of "What is the Talmud?" We cannot pass over this article by merely alluding to it; it deserves our full attention on account of the mischief it had already wrought, and must work, in the minds of those who are not able to correct the erroneous statements contained in it.

The writer accuses [p. 4 of the American reprint, contained in the *Literary Remains* (N. Y., 1874)] the investigators of the Talmud of mistaking the grimy stone caricatures over our cathedrals for the gleaming statues of the saints within. But entering into the cathedrals of the Talmud and beholding these saints, we are told by Rabbi Ilaï, the elder: when men wish to sin let them go to a place where they are unknown, and clothe themselves in black so as not to dis-

---

1. A writer in the *Edinburgh Review* (July, 1873) says : " But brilliant as that essay was, it was superficial. It gave, we think, a very partial view of what the Talmud really is, and it did scant justice to many considerable laborers in the same field of inquiry. Mr. Deutsch spoke as if nobody, before himself, had written anything intelligible on the subject." Mr. Farrar, speaking of works on the Talmud in Latin and German, which never entered into general literature, says, " Had it been otherwise, the mass of English readers would never have been prepared to accept the utterly untenable notions about the Talmud, and the glowing wisdom and exquisite morality by which it was supposed to be pervaded, into which they were betrayed by the learned enthusiasm of the late Dr. Deutsch in his article on the Talmud " (Preface to Hershon's *Talmudic Miscellany*).

honor God openly (*Moëd Katon* fol. 17, col. 1 ; *Hagiga* fol. 16, col. 1 ; *Kiddushim* fol. 40, col. 1). Of the chastity of Rabbi Eliezer ben Dordai we get an idea when we hear that there was not a bad woman in the world, whom he did not go to see " (*Aboda Zarah* fol. 17, col. 1 ¹). Of Rabbi Abbuha we read that he was such a strong eater that a fly could not rest upon his forehead (*Berachoth* fol. 44, col. 1) ; and of Rabbi Ame and Rabbi Asse that they ate so much that the hair fell from their heads, and of Rabbi Simeon, the son of Lakesh, that he ate so much that he lost his senses (*ibid.*), of Rabbi Ismael and Rabbi Eleazar we read that they were so

---

1. These instances were not the exception. For says the writer in the *Edinburgh Review*, already quoted : " On no subject are the doctors of the Talmud so prone to dilate as on that of the relation between the sexes. The third of the six orders of the Talmud, consisting of seven tracts, is entirely occupied with the subject of the rights and duties of women, and of men in relation to women. But in addition to this, questions of the same nature are continually springing forth from the ambush in the Gemara. It is very difficult, however, to convey to the English reader in appropriate language the mode in which that subject is approached by the Jewish doctors of the law. Delicacy, according to our ideas, is to them a thing utterly unknown. For modesty they have neither name nor place. Chastity, as exalted into a virtue by the Roman Church, is esteemed by the Halaca to be violation of a distinct command of the written Law. Virginity after mature years is a stigma if not a sin. With the exception of the prohibition of marriage within certain close limits of consanguinity, which do not forbid a man to take to wife the daughter of his brother or sister, almost the sole duty as to marital relations enforced by the Talmud is the fidelity of a wife to her husband during the existence of the technical marriage tie. The number of wives legal seems to have been limited only by the wealth of the husband ; the rights of contemporary wives up to the number of four being severally discussed in the tract Kedurhin." How loose the marriage-tie was regarded may be seen from the fact that the school of Hillel allowed the divorce of a wife if she over-salted or over roasted her husband's dinner ; and Aqiba allowed it in the case of a man finding a woman fairer in his eyes than his wife. " In a word," says a writer in the *Cornhill Magazine*, " the opinions of the majority of the Rabbis concerning marriage seem to have been as free as those celebrated ones of Cato, whose friendship for Hortensius extended *usque ad aras*, and a little beyond." It will therefore not be surprising to know that the doctors of the Talmud had a very low opinion of the female sex. They put them in the category with slaves and children. Women were not to be instructed in the law, for " you shall teach the law to your sons " and not to your daughters. " He who teaches his daughter the law is like as if he teaches her to sin." " The mind of woman is weak." " The world cannot exist without males and females. but blessed is he whose children are sons : woe to him whose children are daughters." In the morning prayer the husband and son thanks God " that he hath not made him a woman."

corpulent that when they stood face to face
a pair of oxen could pass under them without touching them (*Baba Metsia* fol. 84, col.
1). The Jews, we read, are directed to get
so drunk on the Feast of Purim that they
cannot discern the difference between
" Blessed be Mordecai and cursed be
Haman," and " Cursed be Mordecai and
blessed be Haman." And as an illustration
we read : Rabba and Rabbi Zira made their
Purim entertainment together. When Rabba
got drunk, he arose and killed Rabbi Zira.
On the following day he prayed for mercy,
and restored him to life. The following
year Rabba proposed to him again to make
their Purim entertainment together ; but he
answered, " Miracles don't happen every
day." (*Megilla* fol. 7, col. 2). Of the honesty
of Rabbi Samuel and Rabbi Cahana we read
a nice story in *Baba Kamma* (fol. 113, col. 2),
which we had better pass over, for enough
has been said of some of the Talmudical
saints.

The writer in the *Quarterly*, though he
admits (p. 12) that the Talmud contains
" gross offences against modern taste " yet
endeavors at the same time to apologize for
those parts by telling that, when compared
with other ancient systems of jurisprudence,"
" the Talmud will then stand out rather
favorably than otherwise." It is not necessary to say much on this painful and dis-
gusting part of the subject ; but we will say
this, that it is one thing to point to the existence of mire, that we may warn the unwary, and another to wallow with delight in
it. We heartily wish that some of the
rabbis who wrote the Talmud had been con-
tent with discharging that which may be
considered a duty, and not laid themselves
open to the charge justly brought against

them, of doing injury to the morals and minds of those who study their writings, by their unnecessary and improper statements and details, of which the treatise *Nidda*, which we have here especially in view, and which treats of the "menstruating woman" is so full. When in 1843, Messrs. De Sola and Raphall published a translation of a portion of the Mishna, they excused the omission of this treatise by saying, in the preface to their work, "The treatise *Nidda* not being suited to the refined notions of the English reader, has not been printed." They did well and wisely to omit it in the list of portions selected for translation ; and says the writer in the *Edinburgh Review :* "*Niddah* should be read only by persons bound to study medicine, being devoted to certain rules not ordinarily discussed ; although they appear to have occupied a disproportionate part of the attention of the rab, bins. The objections that our modern sense of propriety raises to the practice of the confessional apply with no less force to the subject of this tract, considered as a matter to be regulated by the priesthood."

Considering the very many bad features of the Talmud, which include also offensive passages,—we must not be astonished at the fact that the Talmud has so often been burned. But in this respect the Talmud has only reaped what it has sowed. It was the Talmud which taught that in case of a fire breaking out on the Sabbath, the gospels should not be rescued. The Talmud is not the only work which has been burned. The Bible has been burned. Why should the Talmud have escaped? Besides, ignorance and fanaticism, in all ages and countries, have burned the books which they supposed were against their system. This was especially the case with the Talmud, A.D. 1240, when a conference was held at Paris between Nicolaus Donin and some Jewish rabbis concerning certain blasphemies contained in the Talmud and written against Jesus and Mary. Rabbi Jechiel, the most prominent of the Jewish rabbis at that conference, would not admit that the Jesus spoken of in the Talmud was Jesus of Nazareth, but another Jesus, a discovery which was copied by later writers. But modern Jews acknowledge the failure of this argument, for, says Dr. Levin, in his prize essay : "we must regard the attempt of R. Jechiel to ascertain that there were two by the name of Jesus as unfortunate, original as the idea may be." [1] The result of his conference was that the Talmud in wagon-loads was burned at Paris in 1242. This was the first attack. In our days, such accusations against the Talmud as that professed by Donin were impossible, because all these offensive passages have been removed—not so much by the hands of the censor, as by the Jews themselves, as the following document or circular letter, addressed by a council of elders, convened in Poland in the Jewish year 5391 (*i.e.*, A.D. 1631), to their co-religionists, which at the same time contains the clew why in later editions of the Talmud certain passages are wanting, will show. The circular runs thus in the translation of Ch. Leslie : [2] "Great peace to our beloved brethren of the house of Israel.—Having received information that many Christians have applied themselves with great care to acquire the knowledge of

---

1. *Die Religions Disputation des R. Jechiel von Paris, etc.*, published in Graetz's *Monatsschrift*, 1860, p. 193.
2. *A Short and Easy Method with the Jews*, p. 2, *seq.* (London, 1812), where the original Hebrew is also found.

the language in which our books are written, we therefore enjoin you, under the penalty of the great ban (to be inflicted upon such of you as shall transgress this our statute), that you do not in any new edition either of the Mishna or Gemara, publish anything relative to Jesus of Nazareth ; and you take special care not to write anything concerning him; either good or bad, so that neither ourselves nor our religion may be exposed to any injury. For we know what those men of Belial, the mumrim, have done to us, when they became Christians, and how their representations against us have obtained credit. Therefore, let this make you cautious. If you should not pay strict attention to this our letter, but act contrary thereto, and continue to publish our books in the same manner as before, you may occasion, both to us and yourselves, greater afflictions than we have hitherto experienced, and be the means of our being compelled to embrace the Christian religion, as we were formerly ; and thus our latter troubles might be worse than the former. For these reasons we command you that, if you publish any new edition of those books, let the places relating to Jesus of Nazareth be left in blank, and fill up the space with a circle like this ○. But the rabbins and teachers of children will know how to instruct the youth by word of mouth. Then Christians will no longer have anything to show against us upon this subject, and we may expect deliverance from the afflictions we have formerly labored under, and reasonably hope to live in peace."

That the Talmud also contains a great many beautiful maxims, good sayings, fine prayers, etc., no one can deny ; it would be strange, indeed, if the 2947 pages should

contain nothing but nonsense. But unless
the whole work be translated, it will never
be known what the Talmud really is. For
says the writer in the *Edinburgh Review :*

"It has proved a grateful and not unrewarded task to
wander through the mazes of the Talmud, and to cull flowers yet sparkling with the very dew of Eden. Figures in
shining garments haunt its recesses. Prayers of deep
devotion, sublime confidence, and noble benediction, echo
in its ancient tongue. Sentiments of lofty courage, of high
resolve, of infantile tenderness, of far-seeing prudence, fall
from the lips of venerable sages. Fairy tales, for Sunday
evenings' recital, go back to early days when there were
giants in the land ; or those, yet earlier, when, as Josephus
tells us, man had a common language with the animals.
Mr. Darwin might write a new book illustrative of a pre-
historic common ancestry, from the fables of Syria, India,
and Greece, that tell of animal wisdom. From the glorious
liturgy of the Temple, Rome and her daughters have stolen
almost all that is sublime in their own, with the one exception of the hymn of St. Ambrose, itself formed on a Jewish
model. Page after page might be filled with such language
and such thought as does not flow from modern pens.
Yet the possessor of these inviting spoils would know but
little of the real character of the Talmud.
"No less practicable would it be to stray with an opposite
intention, and to extract venom, instead of honey, from the
flowers that seem to spring up in self-sown profusion.
Fierce, intolerant, vindictive hatred for mankind, with
small exception—confined in some cases to the singular
number ; idle subtlety, frittering away at once the energy
of the human intellect and the dignity of the divine law ;
pride and self-conceit amounting to insanity ; adulation that
hails a man covered with the rags of a beggar as saint and
prince, and king ; indelicacy pushed to a grossness that
renders what it calls virtue more hateful than the vice of
more modest people ; all those might be strung together in
one black paternoster, and yet they would give no more
just an idea of the Talmud than would the chaplets of its
lovelier flowers. For both are there, and more."

But "What is the Talmud?" In answer
to this question we will subjoin some of the
opinions on the Talmud by different authors.
Thus B. Disraeli in his *Genius of Judaism* (p.
88) says :

"The Mishna, at first considered as the perfection of
human skill and industry, at length was discovered to be
a vast indigested heap of contradictory decisions. It was
a supplement to the law of Moses, which itself required

a supplement. Composed in curt, unconnected sentences, such as would occur in conversation designed to be got by rote by the students from the lips of their oracles, the whole was at length declared not to be even intelligible, and served only to perplex or terrify the scrupulous Hebrew. Such is the nature of 'traditions,' when they are fairly brought together and submitted to the eye.

"The Mishna now only served as a text (the law of Moses being slightly regarded) to call forth interminable expositions. The very sons of the founder of the Mishna set the example by pretending that they understood what their father meant. The work once begun, it was found difficult to get rid of the workmen. The sons of 'the Holy' were succeeded by a long line of other rulers of their divinity schools under the title, aptly descriptive, of the *Amoraim*, or *dictators*. These were the founders of the new despotism; afterwards, wanderers in the labyrinth they had themselves constructed, roved the *Seburaim*, or *opinionists*, no longer dictating but inferring opinions by keen disputations. As in the decline of empire mere florid titles delight, rose the *Geonim*, or *sublime* doctors; till at length, in the dissolution of this dynasty of theologians, they sunk into the familiar titular honor of *Rabbi*, or master !

" The Jews had incurred the solemn reproach in the days of Jesus, of having annihilated the word of God by the load of their *traditions*. The calamity became more fearful when, two centuries after, they received the fatal gift of their collected traditions called *Mishna*, and still more fatal when, in the lapse of the three subsequent centuries, the epoch of the final compilation, was produced the commentary graced with the title of the *Gemara*, completeness or perfection. It was imagined that the human intellect had here touched its meridian. The national mind was completely rabbinised. It became uniform, stable, and peculiar. The Talmud, or the Doctrinal, as the whole is called, was the labor of nearly 500 years.

" Here, then, we find a prodigious mass of contradictory opinions, an infinite number of casuistical cases, a logic of scholastic theology, some recondite wisdom, and much rambling dotage; many puerile tales and oriental fancies; ethics and sophisms, reasonings and unreasonings, subtle solutions, and maxims and riddles: nothing in human life seems to have happened which these doctors have not perplexed or provided against, for their observations are as minute as Swift exhausted in his 'Directions to Servants.' The children of Israel, always children, were delighted as their Talmud increased its volume, and their hardships. The Gemara was a third law to elucidate the Mishna, which was a second law, and which had thrown the first law, the law of Moses, into obscurity."

Dr. Isaac Da Costa, in his *Israel and the Gentiles* (New York, 1855, p. 116), says:

"The Talmud is a most curious monument, raised with astonishing labor, yet made up of puerilities. Like the present position of the Jew, away from his country, far from his Messiah, and in disobedience to his God, the Talmud itself is a chaos in which the most opposite elements are found in juxtaposition. It is a book which seems in some parts entirely devoid of common sense, and in others filled with deep meaning, abounding with absurd subtleties and legal *finesse*, full of foolish tales and wild imaginations; but also containing aphorisms and parables which, except in their lack of the simple and sublime character of the Holy Writ, resemble in a degree the parables and sentences of the New Testament. The Talmud is an immense heap of rubbish, at the bottom of which a few bright pearls of Eastern wisdom are to be found. No book has ever expressed more faithfully the spirit of its authors. This we notice the more when comparing the Talmud with the Bible—the Bible, that Book of books, given *to*, and *by* means of, the Israel of God; the Talmud, the book composed by Israel *without* their God, in the time of their dispersion, their misery, and their degeneracy."

Dr. Milman, in his *History of the Jews* (III. 13), says:

"The reader, at each successive extract from this extraordinary compilation (*i.e.*, the Talmud), hesitates whether to admire the vein of profound allegorical truth and the pleasing moral apologue, to smile at the monstrous extravagance, or to shudder at the daring blasphemy. The influence of the Talmud on European superstitions, opinions, and even literature remains to be traced. To the Jew the Talmud became the magic circle within which the national mind patiently labored for ages in performing the bidding of the ancient and mighty enchanters, who drew the sacred line beyond which it might not venture to pass."

Dr. Farrar, in his *Life of Christ* (II. 485), says:

"Anything more utterly unhistorical than the Talmud cannot be conceived. It is probable that no human writings ever confounded names, dates, and facts with a more absolute indifference. The genius of the Jews is the reverse of what, in these days, we should call historical. . . . Some excellent maxims—even some close parallels to the utterances of Christ—may be quoted, of course, from the Talmud, where they lie imbedded like pearls in ' a sea ' of obscurity and mud. It seems to me indispensable—and a

matter which every one can now verify for himself—that
these are amazingly few, considering the vast bulk of national
literature from which they are drawn. And, after all,
who shall prove to us that these sayings were always uttered
by the rabbis to whom they were attributed? Who
will supply us with the faintest approach to a proof that
(when not founded on the Old Testament) they were not
directly or indirectly due to Christian influence or Christian
thought?"

In his *History of Interpretation* (1886, p.
91, *seq.*, 106), he says:

"The Talmud is one of the strangest of the Bibles of
humanity! It has been called 'the Pandects of Judaism,'
but it is also the encyclopædia of Jewish science, and the
Hansard of nearly a thousand years of discussion in Jewish
schools, and the *Rationale Officiorum* of all its ceremonial.
It is a veritable *lanx satura*. It consists of disputes,
decisions, stories, sermons, legends, scripture comments,
moral truths, prescriptions, observations, mazes of legal
enactments, gorgeous day-dreams, masked history, ill-disguised
rationalism. It is drawn from the promiscuous note-books
of students of very diverse attainments and character
in which they have scribbled down all the wisdom and all
the unwisdom, all the sense and all the nonsense which
was talked for centuries in the schools of all kinds of Rabbis.
The Jew might say of his beloved Rabbi,

'Quicquid agunt homines, votum, timor, ira, voluptas,
Gaudia, discursus, nostri est farrago libelli.'

"The work of hundreds of learned men of different ages,
countries, and conditions, it forms a wonderful monument
of human industry, human wisdom, and human folly.
Written in a style of lapidary brevity, it reads like a collection
of telegraphic messages. It is also full of uncouth
grammar, barbarous solecisms, and exotic words. We can
hardly wonder that it is difficult to discover the method of
its apparently confused and desultory discussions, when we
remember that it was developed amid conditions of peril
and discouragement, amid endless disturbances of war and
violences of persecution, under the jealous eyes of the Roman
informers or the cruel greed and fanatical malice of
Persian oppressors. Such being its origin it naturally
teems with errors, exaggerations, and even obscurities;
with strange superstitions of Eastern demonology; with
wild Arabian tales about the freaks of Ashmodai; with
childish extravagances of fancy about Behemoth and the
bird Bar Juchne and the Shorhabor: with perverted logic;
with confusions of genealogy, chronology, and history;
with exorcisms, incantations, and magic formulæ; with
profane and old wives' fables, of which some few may have
had a hidden significance to those who had the key to their

meaning, but of which the majority were understood by the multitude in their literal absurdity.

"These 'Jewish myths and genealogies,' as St. Paul calls them, have their dark side. All that can be urged by way of excuse for their baser elements is that they were not always meant to be taken literally, or to be weighed in jeweller's scales. The Rabbi, talking familiarly in his lighter and unguarded moments did not intend his eager pupils to retain and record his most rash and accidental utterances. Here, however, in this strange literary Herculaneum all things are swept together in wild confusion. Things grave and fantastic, great and small, valuable and worthless, Jewish and Pagan, the altar and its ashes are piled together in wild disorder. Amid the labyrinths of rubbish we require a torch to enable us to pick up an accidental gem.

"Such gems, indeed, it contains. In this sea of the Talmud—'this strange, wild, weird ocean, with its leviathans, and its wrecks of golden argosies, and its forlorn bells, which send up their dreamy sounds ever and anon' —there are some treasures, which have frequently been gathered amid the froth and scum, the flotsam and jetsam of a thousand years. Exquisite parables and noble aphorisms are scattered in its pages here and there. The general darkness is sometimes broken by keen flashes of intellectual, and even of spiritual light. But these are rare, and to speak of the Talmud in such terms of enthusiasm as those with which Dr. Deutsch charmed the unwary, or to say of it, with Professor Hurwitz, that no uninspired work contains more interesting, more varied, or more valuable information,—is to be blinded by national prejudice to facts which any one can put to the test.

"But the worst result of the influence exercised by the Talmud is the injury which it inflicted on the living oracle of God. We should be paying to Talmudism too high a compliment were we to say that it is like

> 'The pleached bower,
> Where honeysuckles ripened by the sun
> Forbid the sun to enter.'

"The most distinctive flowers of the Talmud are artificial flowers—flowers by which we cannot for a moment be deceived."

Prof. Delitzsch in his *Jüdisches Handwerkerleben zur Zeit Jesu*,[1] says:

"Those who have not in some degree accomplished the extremely difficult task of reading this work for themselves will hardly be able to form a clear idea of this polynominal colossus. It is a vast debating club, in which there hum

---

1. 3d ed. Erlangen 1879, p. 35. (English translation by Rev. B. Pick, New York, 1883, p. 37, *seq.*)

confusedly the myriad voices of at least five centuries. As we all know by experience, a law, though very minutely and exactly defined, may yet be susceptible of various interpretations, and question on question is sure to arise when it comes to be applied to the ever-varying circumstances of actual life. Suppose, then, you have about ten thousand legal definitions all relating to Jewish life, and classified under different heads, and add to these ten thousand definitions about five hundred doctors and lawyers, belonging mostly to Palestine or Babylonia, who make these definitions, one after the other, the subject of examination and debate, and who, with hair-splitting acuteness exhaust not only every possible sense the words will bear, but every possible practical occurrence arising out of them. Suppose that these fine-spun threads of these legal disquisitions frequently lose themselves in digressions, and that, when one has waded through a long tract of this sandy desert, one lights, here and there, on some green oasis consisting of stories and sayings of universal interest. This done, you will have some tolerable idea of this enormous and, in its way, unique code of laws, in comparison with which, in point of comprehensiveness, the law-books of all other nations are but lilliputian ; and, when compared with the hum of its kaleidoscopic Babel, they resemble, indeed, calm and studious retreat."

Dr. Geikie in his *Life and Works of Christ* (New York, 1881, vol. II, p. 618), says :

"It would be strange indeed, if in the interminable dust-heaps of the Talmud, of which the Babylonian alone, including the Rabbinical commentaries on it, fill twenty-four volumes folio (Venice, 1682), did not contain some stray pearls. Among the many Rabbis of successive centuries, whose sayings are reported in it, or whose expositions are appended to it, there was here and there a man of genius, or of pure and lofty aspirations who has left traces of his finer or more religious nature in sayings well worthy preservation. But glimpses of profound metaphysics, stray parables of real beauty, and occasional sentiments of true spiritual breath and elevation, are only the rare grains of wheat in mountains of chaff."

Dr. Edersheim in *Life and Times of Jesus the Messiah* (London, 1883), vol. I, p. 103, says :

"If we imagine something combining law reports, a Rabbinical 'Hansard,' and notes of a theological debating club—all thoroughly oriental, full of digressions, anecdotes, quaint sayings, fancies, legend, and too often of what, from its profanity, superstition and even obscenity, could scarcely be quoted, we may form some general idea of what the Talmud is."

Dr. Schaff in *History of the Christian Church* (New York, 1883) vol. II., pp. 38, 39, says :

"The Talmud is the slow growth of several centuries. It is a chaos of Jewish learning, wisdom, and folly, a continent of rubbish, with hidden pearls of true maxims and poetic parables. It is the Old Testament misinterpreted and turned against the New, in fact, though not in form. It is a Rabbinical Bible without inspiration, without the Messiah, without hope. It shares the tenacity of the Jewish race, and, like it, continues involuntarily to bear testimony to the truth of Christianity. . . . The Talmud is the Bible of Judaism separated from, and hostile to, Christianity, but it barely notices it except indirectly. It completed the isolation of the Jews from all other people."

In connection with the last sentence of Dr. Schaff, we quote the following from the article " The Talmud " in the " *Edinburgh Review*, July, 1873 :

"But when we sound the sombre, exclusive, pitiless depths of the inner doctrine of the Talmud, we see that a reason exists for that marked and secular demarcation between the Jew and the Gentile, for which we were about to blame our own intolerance. Purposely and rigidly, in exile no less than in the splendor of the theocratic polity, has the hand of the Jew been directed by the depositaries of his traditions against every man. It is the law of self-defence that has raised the hand of every man against him. Our ancestors were not, after all, so blindly cruel as some writers are too ready to admit. Offers of friendship and of brotherhood are as powerless as are the fires of the Inquisition to break down that moral wall, substantial as the very fortress wall of the Temple, that resisted the voice of Christ, and that has been strengthened by the constant efforts of the doctors of the Talmud for five centuries after the fall of Jerusalem. The power of resistance is the same at this moment that it was two thousand years ago. The point of attack is still the same as in the days of Herod. To the question, 'Who is my neighbor?' the Talmud returns one reply, and the parable of the Good Samaritan another. The mercy to be shown, as Moses taught, to the stranger, is qualified by the Halaca by the assumption that he must also be a proselyte. All questions as to which accord would be otherwise possible, whether in the historic past, or the dimly predicted future, are insoluble, while the justice, mercy, and truth—

he weightier matters of the Law—are, by the guardians of
he Law of Moses, confined to those of their own faith and
)lood. The vitality of Judaism was contained in the doc-
rine, that the Jews had one father, even God. The hope
)f the future of humanity lies in the good tidings that God
s the common Father of mankind."

Mr. Alexander, in his book on *The Jews*;
'heir Past, Present and Future (London, 1870):

"The Talmud, as it now stands, is almost the whole liter-
ture of the Jews during a thousand years. Commentator
ollowed upon commentator, till at last the whole became
n immense bulk, the original Babylonian Talmud alone
:onsisting of 2, 947 folio pages. Out of such a literature
t is easy to make quotations which may throw an odium
)ver the whole. But fancy if the production of a thousand
years of English literature, say, from the 'History' of the
venerable Bede to Milton's 'Paradise Lost,' were thrown
:ogether into a number of uniform folios, and judged in
like manner; if because some superstitious monks wrote
silly 'Lives of Saints,' therefore the works of John Bun-
yan should also be considered worthless. The absurdity is
too obvious to require another word from me. Such, however, is the continual treatment the Talmud receives both at
the hand of its friends and of its enemies. Both will find it
easy to quote in behalf of their preconceived notions, but
the earnest student will rather try to weigh the matter im-
partially, retain the good he can find even in the Talmud,
and reject what will not stand the test of God's Word."

In conclusion, while we acknowledge the
fact that this great encyclopædia of Hebrew
wisdom teems with error and that in almost
every department in science, in natural history, in chronology, genealogy, logic, and
morals, falsehood and mistake are mixed up
with truth upon its pages, we should never-
theless confess, that, notwithstanding, with
all its imperfections, it is a useful book, an
attestation of the past, a criterion of progress
already attained, and a prophecy of the
future.

"It is a witness too, of the lengths of folly to which
the mind of man may drift when he disdains the wisdom
of God as revealed in the Gospel, and in these respects
it will always have a claim on the attention of the wise.
When Talmudism, as a religious system, shall in a

generation or two have passed away, the Talmud itself will be still resorted to as a treasury of things amusing and things profitable ; a deep cavern of antiquity, where he who carries the necessary torch will not fail to find, amid whole labyrinths of the rubbish of times gone by, those inestimable lessons that will be true for all times to come, and gems of ethical and poetic thought which retain their brightness forever."—ETHERIDGE, *Introduction to Jewish Literature.*

LITERARY USE.

The Talmud has been applied to the criticism and interpretation of the OLD TESTAMENT. Most of its citations, however, agree with the present masoretic text. It has probably been conformed to the masoretic standard by the rabbins, at least in the later editions. Besides it is very strange that in relation to the Pentateuch the other books of the Old Testament are almost entirely ignored. As for the interpretation of the Talmud, with its endless canons and artificial rules, Dr. Farrar is correct when he says, "The actual exegesis of Scripture in which the Talmud abounds is so arbitrary and so futile, so tasteless and so insincere, that it must have given to its students a radically false conception of their sacred books. It represented to them the Law of Moses as fragmentary without the supplement of tradition, and inexplicable without the intervention of Rabbinism. The Jews were taught to care more for it (the Talmud), and to devote more continued study to its masses of casuistry and extravagance than to the divine beauty of the Psalms and the noble moral teaching of the Prophets. Thus they were turned from the river of life to broken cisterns which could hold no water, or only the shallow and stagnant pool of a tradition polluted by a thousand strange and heterogeneous influences. A "Biblical theologian" was as great an object of contempt to the Rabbis as he became to the schoolmen in their worst epoch of decline." [1]

A valuable witness, however, is the Talmud as to the state of the Old Testament as it was in the time of the Talmud. And in this respect it may be said that the state of the text was then almost the same as it is now, that is to say, that most of the masoretic apparatus is already mentioned in the Talmud. We also find some incidental notes concerning the Septuagint and the changes introduced by the translators, also notices concerning the canonicity of some books of the Old Testament. All these and the like notices come in incidentally.

Since the Old Testament speaks of the promised Messiah, it is of great interest to know what the Talmud has to say on that point. And here we must remark at once that all the notices concerning the Messiah are of post-Christian date. The Mishna has nothing to say about the Messiah ;—the passage in Sotah which speaks of the signs of the approaching Messiah does not originally belong to the Mishna.

NOTICES CONCERNING THE MESSIAH.

The *locus classicus* is found in the treatise *Sanhedrin* where the last two lines of fol. 96, col. 2, open as follows: "Rav Nachman [2] said to Rav Yitzchak: Hast thou heard when Bar-Naphli [*i. e.*, the son of the fallen] comes? He replied: Who is Bar-Naphli? He answered, Messiah. But dost thou call the Messiah Bar-Naphli? He said,

1. *History of Interpretation*, p. 94.
2. This rabbi, whose full name is R. Nachman ben Jacob, died A.D. 320. Of him we are told (*Yebamoth* fol. 37. col. 2, and *Yoma* fol. 18, col. 2.) that whenever he came to Shachanziv he would ask by proclamation whether any woman would be willing to be his wife during his stay there. The same we read *l. c.* of Rav, whenever he came on a visit to Dardashir !

Yes, for it is written: "In that day will I
raise up (fol. 97, col. 1) the tabernacle of
David that is fallen (*han-nophclcth.* Amos
ix. 11.¹) He said to him, Thus said Rabbi
Jochanan, ² The generation in which the son
of David ³ will come, therein shall the disciples of the wise grow fewer and fewer;
and as to the rest, their eyes shall be con-
sumed by trouble and groaning, and afflictions shall be multiplied, and vexatious decrees shall be renewed; whilst the first is
being ordered, the second will hasten to
come."

The rabbis have taught: In the cycle of
seven years in which the son of David shall
come, in its first year this passage will be
confirmed: "I shall cause rain to come
upon one city, and upon another city I shall
not cause the rain to come " (Amos iv. 7); in
the second the arrows of famine shall be sent
forth; in the third there shall be a great
famine, and men, and women, and children
shall die, saints and wonder-workers, and
the law shall be forgotten by those who
studied it; in the fourth shall be plenty, and
yet no plenty; in the fifth shall be great
plenty, and they shall eat and drink, and
rejoice, and the law shall return to those
who studied it; in the sixth there shall be
rumors [*i.e.*, of the coming Messiah]; in the

---

1. Comp. Acts xv. 16, where James quotes the same passage as
Messianic.
2. Better known as Jochanan bar Napha, *i.e.*, the son of a blacksmith, died A.D. 278.
3. Son of David. This name occurs very often in the Talmud
for the Messiah. Often only "David," without the addition of
"son" is given, as in *Rosh-ha-shanah*, fol. 25, col. 1, where we
read : "David, the King of Israel, lives and remains forever."
Levy in his *Neuhebr. Wörterbuch* s. v. *David*, in quoting this
passage says that it is probably a negation of the alleged Messiahship of Jesus (Δαβίδ ὁ Χριστός ὁ Βασιλεύς τοῦ Ἰσραήλ, Matt. xx.,
30, 31, Mark xv., 32), who was killed, and to whom eternal life was
denied (sic!). But what sense is there when the Orthodox Jews
to this day use the very same words, "David, the King of Israel,
lives and remains forever," in their prayer at the appearance of
the new moon ?

seventh there shall be wars ; at the end of
the seventh the son of David shall come.
R. Joseph said: there have been many
weeks of this kind, and he has not come.
Abaye said, in the sixth year rumors, in the
· seventh wars ; has it been so yet? and further, have the other events happened in the
order here laid down? We have the teaching, R. Judah said, in the generation in
which the son of David shall come, the
house of assembly will be for fornication,
and Galilee shall be in ruins, and Gaban laid
waste, and tne men of Gebul shall go from
city to city, and shall find no favor. And
the wisdom of the scribes shall stink, and
they that fear sin shall be despised, and the
face of that generation shall be [shameless]
as that of a dog ; truth shall fail as it is said :
" Yea, truth faileth " (Isa. lix. 15), and he
that turns from evil will be regarded as a
fool. What is the meaning : " Yea, truth
faileth ? " Those of the house of Rab say,
that she shall be made into droves [*i. e.*,
divided among opposing schools or parties]
and thus go away. What is the meaning of:
He that turns from evil will be regarded as a
fool? Those of the house of R. Shilah say,
every one that departed from evil shall be
counted a fool by the world.

We have the teaching: R. Nehoraï says,
in the generation in which the son of David
shall come, the young men shall make
ashamed the countenances of old men ; old
men shall stand up in the presence of young
men ; and the daughter will rise against her
mother, and the daughter-in-law against her
mother-in-law, and the face of that generation shall be as the face of a dog, and the
son will have no reverence for his father.

We have the teaching: R. Nehemiah says,
in the generation in which the son of David

shall come, impudence shall increase, and he that will be honored, shall be an unrighteous man; the vine will produce its fruit, but wine will be dear, and the kingdom will turn itself to heresy, and there will be no reproof.* This supports R. Isaac, who said: the son of David shall not come till the whole kingdom is turned to heresy. Raba said: where is that said [in Scripture]? [Answer] When " it is all turned white [i. e., leprous] the man is clean " (Lev. xiii. 13).

The rabbis have taught: " For the Lord shall judge his people," etc., "when he seeth that power is gone, and there is none shut up or left" (Deut. xxxii. 36), the son of David cometh not till informers increase. Another meaning is: till disciples diminish. Another meaning is: till the farthing disappears from the purse. Another meaning is: till men begin to give up all hope of redemption, for it is said, "and there is none shut up or left," and if it were possible, there is none that upholdeth and aideth Israel. This [last interpretation] is like that [saying] of R. Zera, who upon finding the rabbis busied with that question [viz.: of Messiah's coming] said to them: I pray you put not the time further back, for we have a tradition: three things—Messiah, a find, and a scorpion.

---

* A similar description of the signs of the last times is also given in the Treatise *Sotah* fol. 49, col. 2: In the foot-prints of the Messiah, impudence will increase, an l there will be dearness [or scarcity]. The vine will produce its fruit, but wine will be dear. And the kingdom [i.e. the government] will turn itself to heresy [i.e. to Christianity] and there will be no reproof. And the house of the assembly will be for fornication. Galilee will be destroyed, and Gablan laid waste. The men of Gebul will go from city to city, and find no favor. The wisdom of the scribes will stink, and those who fear sin will be despise l, and truth will fail. Bovs will whiten [i.e. confuse] the faces of old men ; and old men will rise up before the young. The son will treat the father shamefully, and the daughter will rise up against her mother, and the daughter-in-law against the mother-in-law, and a man's foes will be those of his own household, the face of that generation will be as the face of a dog ; the son will have no shame before his father. Upon whom then are we to trust ? Upon our Father, which is in Heaven.

R. Ketina said : the world is to last 6000 years, and for 1000 it shall lie in ruins, for it is said : " and the Lord alone shall be exalted in that day (Isa. ii. 11). Abaye said : for 2000 it will lie waste, for it is said : " He will vivify us for two days, on the third day he will raise us up, and we shall live in his sight" (Hos. vi. 2). The opinion of R. Ketina is supported as follows : As in the heptad there is one year of remission, so likewise in that age there will be a remission of a thousand years in seven thousand years, for it is said: "And the Lord alone shall be exalted in that day," and it is also said: "A psalm of singing for the Sabbath day " (Ps. xcii. 1), a day which shall be altogether Sabbath, and it is also said : a thousand years in thy sight are but as yesterday, when it is past (Ps. xc. 4).

Tradition of the school of Elijah : the world is to stand 6000 years ; two thousand years confusion, two thousand the law, two thousand the days of Messiah (fol. 97, col. 2), but on account of our sins, which have so multiplied, there have elapsed of them so many as have already elapsed [without Messiah appearing].

Eliyahu said to Rav Judah, brother of Rav Sallah, the pious : the world cannot last less than eighty-five jubilees [*i. e.*, 4165 years], and in the last jubilee the son of David comes.

At the beginning or at the end of it ? He replied : I know not.

Will [the whole time] have already passed or not : I know not.

Rav Ashé said. thus had he spoken to me : until that time expect him not ; from that time onward expect him.

Rav Chanan, the son of Tachlipha, sent word to Rav Joseph : I have found a man with a scroll in his hand, written with Assyrian

letters, but in the sacred tongue, and I asked
him whence didst thou get it? and he replied : I was a hired soldier in the Persian
army, and I found it among the Persian
treasures. And in this book was written:
four thousand two hundred and ninety-one
years after the creation of the world, the
world shall cease; some of the intervening
years shall be spent in wars of dragons, some
in wars of Gog and Magog, and the rest shall
be the days of Messiah ; and the Holy One
—blessed be his name—shall not renew this
world till after seven thousand years.

R. Acha, son of Raba, says: after 5000
years, so runs our tradition.

There is a teaching : R. Nathan said : this
scripture penetrates down into the abyss [*i. e.*,
is of the deepest import]: " For the vision is
yet for an appointed time, but at the end it
shall speak and not lie ; though it tarry, wait
for it ; because it will surely come, it will
not tarry behind (Hab. ii. 3) not [do] as [did]
our teachers who were inquiring concerning
"until a time, and times and the dividing of
a time " (Dan. vii. 25); nor like R. Simlaï,
who was inquiring concerning " Thou feedest
them with the bread of tears; thou makest
them drink of weeping in a threefold measure " (Ps. lxxx. 6) ; nor like R. Aqiba, who
was inquiring : " Yet once, it is a little while
and I will shake the heavens and the earth "
(Hag. ii. 5); but the first kingdom [*i. e.*, that
of the Maccabees] was of seventy years' [du-
ration], the second kingdom [that of Herod]
of fifty-two years, and the kingdom of Ben
Coziba [*i. e.*, son of a lie] two years and a
half, what [meaneth then] He shall breathe
forth for the end, and will not lie? R.
Samuel, son of Nachmani, said that R. Jonathan said : May the bones of those who com-
pute the latter days [when Messiah shall ap-

pear] be blown ; for some say, because the time [of Messiah] has come and Himself has not, therefore He will never come. But wait thou for Him, as it is said : " Though He tarry, wait for Him " (Hab. ii. 3). Perhaps you will say, we wait, but He does not wait ; learn rather to say " and therefore will the Lord wait, that He may be gracious unto you ; and therefore will He be exalted, that He may have mercy upon you " (Isa. xxx. 18). But now, seeing that both we are waiting and He waiteth, what prevents [the coming] ? The [divine] quality of judgment hinders. But as the [divine] quality of judgment hinders, why do we still wait ? [Answer] to receive reward, for it is said : " Blessed are all they that wait for him " (Isa. xxx. 18).

Rav said : all the appointed times are long since past, and the thing depends only on penitence and good works. Samuel said, it is enough that the mourner remain in his mourning [*i. e.*, the final deliverance will not be brought about by Israel's good works, but by God's sole mercy, who mourns in and with his people], as the tradition is.

R. Eliezer, said, if Israel do repentance they will be redeemed, but if not, they will not be redeemed.

R. Joshua replied : If they do not repent they will not be redeemed, but God will raise up to them a king whose decrees shall be as dreadful as Haman, and then Israel will repent and thus he will bring them back to what is good.

Another tradition. R. Eliezer said : If Israel do repentance, they shall be redeemed, for it is said : "Turn, oh backsliding children ; I will heal your backsliding " (Jer. iii. 22). R. Joshua replied, But was it not said long since : " Ye have sold yourselves for nought ;

and ye shall be redeemed without money"
(Isa. lv. 3). Where the words "sold for
nought" meant for idolatry; and the words
"redeemed without money" signify not for
money and good works. R. Eliezer then
said to Rabbi Joshua, But has it not been
said long since : " Return unto me, and I will
return unto you" (Mal. iii. 7). R. Joshua replied, But has it not been said long since,
" I am married unto you, and I will take you
one of a city, and two of a family, and I will
bring you to Zion " (Jer. iii. 14). R. Eliezer
said, But has it not been written long since,
" In returning and rest ye shall be saved?"
(Isa. xxx. 15). R. Joshua replied to Rabbi
Eliezer, But has it not been said long ago :
"Thus saith the Lord, the Redeemer of
Israel and His Holy One, to him whom man
despiseth, to him whom the nation abhoreth,
to a servant of rulers (fol. 98, col. 1), kings
shall see and arise, princes shall worship"
(Isa. xlix. 7). R. Eliezer said to him again,
But has it not been said long ago, " If thou
wilt return, Oh, Israel, return unto me "
(Jer. iv. 1). To which R. Joshua replied,
But has it not been written long ago, " I
heard the man clothed in linen, which was
upon the waters of the river, when he held
up his right hand and his left hand unto
heaven, and sware by Him that liveth forever that it shall be for a time and times and
half a time ; and when he shall have accomplished to scatter the power of the holy people, all these things shall be finished " (Dan.
xii. 7). Whereupon R. Eliezer was silent.

R. Chanina said : The son of David will
not come till fish will not be found even
when required for a sick man ; for it is said :
" Then will I cause their waters to sink, and
their rivers to run like oil" (Eze. xxxii. 14),

and "in that day will I cause the horn of Israel to bud " (Eze. xxix. 21).

Rav Chama, the son of R. Chanina, said : " The son of David will not come till the kingdom will entirely cease in Israel, for it is said : " he shall both cut off the sprigs with pruning hooks " (Isa. xviii. 5), and again, " In that time shall the present be brought unto the Lord of hosts of a people scattered and peeled " (v. 7).

Zeïri said in the name of R. Chanina : The son of David will not come till the proud ones have disappeared from Israel, for it is said : " For then will I take away out of the midst of thee them that rejoice in thy pride " (Zeph. iii. 11), and " I will also leave in the midst of thee an afflicted and poor people, and they shall trust in the name of the Lord " (v. 12).

R. Simlaï said in the name of R. Eliezer the son of R. Simeon : The son of David will not come till all judges and officers shall cease in Israel ; for it is said : " I will restore thy judges as at first, and thy counsellors as at the beginning " (Isa. i. 26).

R. Jochanan said : If thou seest a generation, whose prosperity is gradually diminishing, look out for Him, for it is said : " And the afflicted people thou wilt save " (2 Sam. xii. 28). R. Jochanan also said : If thou seest a generation overwhelmed with great calamities, as with a flood look out for Him ; for it is said : " When the enemy shall come like a flood . . . . the Redeemer shall come to Zion " (Isa. lix. 19, 20). And R. Jochanan further said : The son of David will come only in a generation which is either wholly guiltless, or wholly guilty ; as for the first it is written : " Thy people shall be all righteous : they shall inherit the land forever " (Isa. lx. 21), and as for the latter it is written: "and he saw that there was no man, and wondered that there was no intercessor" (Isa. lix. 16), and it is added: " for mine own sake will I do it " (xlviii. 11).

R. Alexander said of R. Joshua, the son of Levi, who remarked: In one place it is written " Behold, one like the son of man came with the clouds of heaven" (Dan. vii. 17), and in another: " Lowly and riding upon an ass " (Zec. ix. 9). [How is this to be understood? and he answered:] if they will be worthy, He will come with the cloud of heaven ; if not He will come lowly and riding upon an ass. King Shevur [probably Sapor A.D. 250] said to Samuel: You say, Messiah will come on an ass, I will send him my fleet steed. He replied: hast thou one of a hundred colors? [because the ass of the Messiah has so many colors].

R. Joshua, the son of Levi, found Elijah standing at the door of the cave of R. Simon, the son of Yochai, and said to him : shall I arrive at the world to come? He replied: if this the Lord will. R. Joshua, the son of Levi, said, I see two but I hear the voice of three. He also asked: when will Messiah come? Elijah replied, go and ask himself. R. Joshua then said, where does he sit ? At the gate of the city. And how is he to be known? He is sitting among the poor and sick, and they open their wounds and bind them up again all at once ; but he opens only one, and then he opens another, for he thinks, perhaps I may be wanted, and then I must not be delayed. R. Joshua went to him, and said : Peace be upon thee, my master and my Lord. He replied, Peace be upon thee, son of Levi. The rabbi then asked him : when will my Lord come? He replied, To-day. R. Joshua went back to Elijah, who asked him : what did he [Messiah] say to thee? He replied: Peace be upon thee, son of Levi: to which Elijah said: By this he has assured thee and thy father of the world to come. R. Joshua said: He has deceived me, for he said to me, that he will come to-day and yet he did not come. Elijah said to him, he said to thee "to-day," that is, "to-day if ye will hear his voice" (Ps. xci. 7).

The disciples of R. José the son of Kisma, asked: When will the son of David come? He replied: I am afraid that you might ask of me a sign. They replied: We will not ask of thee a sign. He then said to them: When this gate falls and is rebuilt and falls again and they cannot rebuild it, then the son of David will come.

(Fol. 98 col. 2). Rav said: The son of David will not come until the ungodly kingdom has spread itself for a period of nine months over Israel, for it is said: "Therefore will He give them up until the time of a child-bearing woman hath brought forth, and the rest of His brethren shall return unto the children of Israel" (Mic. v. 3).

Ulla said: "Let the Messiah come but may I never see it." The same also, said Rava.

Rav Joseph said, "Let Him come! and I may be counted worthy to sit even under the shadow of the dung of His ass."

Abaii asked Rava, "Why [wouldest thou not care to see the time of the Messiah's coming]?" Is it because of the pains of the Messiah? [There is a remedy] for we have the teaching that the disciples of Rabbi Eliezer asked him, What is a man to do that he may be delivered from the pains of the Messiah? [Answer] Let him diligently occupy himself with the Law and with benevolence.

Rav said, the world was only created for

the sake of David; Samuel said, for the
sake of Moses. Rabbi Jochanan said, only
for the sake of Messiah. What is his name?
Those of the school of Rabbi Shiloh said:
Shiloh is his name, for it is said: "until Shiloh come" (Gen. xlix. 10). Those of the
school of Jannai said: Yinnon is his name,
for it is said: "His name shall endure forever; his name shall be continued (ינון שמו)
as long as the sun" (Ps. lxxii. 17); Those of
the school of R. Chanina said: Chanina is
his name, for it is said: "where I will not
shew you favor" (Jer. xvi. 13). Some say,
Menahem [*i. e.*, comforter], the son of His-
kiah, is his name, for it is said: "the com-
forter that should relieve my soul is far from
me" (Lam. i. 16). But the rabbis say: the
leper of the house of Rabbi is his name, for
it is said: "surely he hath borne our griefs,
and carried our sorrows; yet we did esteem
him stricken, smitten of God, and afflicted"
(Isa. liii. 4).

Rav Nachman said: If there be any like
Him among the living, it is I, for it is said:
"This exalted one shall be of itself, and its
ruler shall proceed from its midst" (Jer.
xxx. 21).

Rav Jehuda said that Rav said: God will
raise up for them another David, as it is
said: "They shall serve the Lord their God,
and David their king, whom I will raise up
until then" (Jer. xxx. 9). But, demanded
Rav Papa of Abaii, is it not written: "My
servant David shall be their prince forever"?
(Eze. xxxvii. 25). [Reply] That is like a
Cæsar and a demi-Cæsar.

Rabbi Simlaï thus expounded: "Woe
unto you that desire the day of the Lord!
to what end is it for you? the day of the
Lord is darkness, and not light" (Am. v.
18). A cock and a bat were once waiting
for the light, when the former said to the

latter : I wait for the light because it is intended for me ; but of what use will it be to
thee? (fol. 99, col. 1). This (adds the nar-
rator) is similar to the reply given by Rabbi
Abuhu to a certain Christian, who had asked
him : When will Messiah come? He replied : When darkness will cover your
people. Why dost thou curse me? asked
the other. The Rabbi answered : Scripture
says so : " For, behold, the darkness shall
cover the earth, and gross darkness the people ; but the Lord shall arise upon thee, and
his glory shall be seen upon thee " (Isa. lx. 2).

Rabbi Eliezer says, The days of the Messiah will be forty years, because it is said
" forty years was I grieved with this generation " (Ps. xcv. 10). Rabbi Eleazar ben Azariah said seventy years, because it is said :
" It shall come to pass in that day, that
Tyre shall be forgotten seventy years according to the days of *one* king (Isa. xxiii.
15). Who is that *one* king? [Reply] The
Messiah. Rabbi says, three generations, for
it is said : " They shall fear thee as long as
the sun and moon endure, from generation
to generation " (Ps. lxxii. 5).

Rabbi Hillel says : " There will be no
Messiah for Israel, because they have enjoyed (fol. 99, col. 1) him already in the
days of Hezekiah." Said Rav Joseph, may
God pardon R. Hillel. When was Hezekiah? In the first house, but Zechariah
prophesied in the second house, and said :
" Rejoice greatly, O daughter of Zion ;
shout, O daughter of Jerusalem ; behold,
thy king cometh unto thee : he is just and
having salvation ; lowly and riding upon an
ass, and upon a colt the foal of an ass "
(Zech. ix. 9).[1]

---

[1]. Farrar (*History of Interpretation,* p. 67) applies this saying to
Hillel the Great, but we doubt the correctness of this application.

Rabbi Eliezer says, the days of the Messiah are forty years; for in one place it is written: "and he suffered thee to hunger, and fed thee" (Deut. viii. 3), and in another place it is written: "Make us glad according to the days wherein thou hast afflicted us, and the years wherein we have seen evil" (Ps. xc. 15).

Rabbi Dosa said, Four hundred years, because it is written: "They shall afflict them four hundred years" (Gen. xv. 13) and in another place: "Make us glad according to the days wherein thou hast afflicted us."

Rabbi says, Three hundred and sixty-five years, according to the number of the days of the sun, for it is said: "The day of vengeance is in mine heart, and the year of my redeemed is come" (Isa. lxiii. 4).

Abimi, the son of Rabbi Abuhu, teaches, the days of the Messiah for Israel are seven thousand years, because it is said: "As the bridegroom rejoiceth over the bride, so shall thy God rejoice over thee" (Isa. lxii. 5).

Rav Nachman bar Yitzchak says, as from the days of Noah down to this time, for it is said: "For this as the days of Noah unto me: for as I have sworn that the waters of Noah," etc. (Isa. liv. 9).

Rabbi Chiya, the son of Abba, said, R. Jochanan said: All the prophets prophesied only with reference to the days of the Messiah: but as regards the world to come, "Eye hath not seen, O Lord, beside thee; what he will do for him that waiteth for him" (Isa. lxiv. 3). This militates against Samuel, who said that the difference between this age and the days of the Messiah, consists only in the cessation of [Israel's] subjection to the Kingdoms.

PART II.
THE TALMUD ON JESUS.

I. THE NAME.

"THE name of Jesus," says Farrar, " occurs some twenty times only in unexpur-
gated editions of the Talmud, the last of
which appeared at Amsterdam in 1645. The
allusions to Him are characterized by intense hatred, disguised by intense fear. They
are also marked by all the gross and reckless
carelessness of these utterly uncritical and
unhistorical writers." [1]   In the Talmud different names are given to Jesus, viz.:

1. JESUS and THE NAZARENE.   Thus we
read, *Sota* fol. 47, col. 1: Our rabbis have
taught: Let the right hand always attract
him again, whom the left has repelled ; not
like Elisha who repelled Gehazi with his two
hands [and not like Joshua ben Perachya who
repelled the Nazarene with his two hands]. [2]
As for Joshua ben Perachya, the following
story is related on the same page, which,
however, we give according to the more complete version in *Sanhedrin* fol. 107, col. 2.
[After the slaughter of the rabbis by order
of King Jannai, Rabbi Joshua, the son of
Perachya, fled with Jesus to Alexandria in
Egypt.   When peace was restored, Simeon,

---

1. *Life of Christ*, II., p. 452.
2. The words within brackets are not in the present editions of the
Talmud.   This applies to all words thus bracketed.   Wünsche, *Der
Babylonische Talmud* (vol. II., p. 340), also remarks that these
words of Sota fol. 47, col. 1, are wanting in our editions.
8

the son of Shetach, sent an epistle to Joshua, with the following contents : " From me, Jerusalem, the holy city, to thee, Alexandria in Egypt. My sister, my husband lives in the midst of thee, and I mourn desolate and lonely." At this, Joshua betook himself to return, and on the way he stopped at an inn, where he was greatly honored. " What a fine inn is this!" said the rabbi. He [Jesus] said : " Her eyes are sore." At this the rabbi said : "Thou impious fellow, do you pay attention to such things?" He brought four hundred trumpets, and excommunicated him. He [Jesus] asked very often to be re-admitted again, but in vain. One day. when the rabbi recited the words, "Hear, O Israel!" Jesus appeared again before him. The rabbi made signs; but Jesus, misunderstanding them, thought the rabbi did not care for him. At this, Jesus turned away, and erected an altar, and bowed before it. When the rabbi told him to repent, Jesus answered : I have learned from thee this doctrine : " Whoever sinneth and causeth others to sin can never repent." And said Mar : Jesus was a sorcerer and seduced and misled [Israel]. This story evidently proves that the rabbis knew of the flight of Jesus into Egypt, although the occurrence is an anachronism, for Joshua lived a century before Christ.

In the treatise *Gittin* fol. 56, col. 2, 57, col. *a*, we read the following filthy story : " Onkelos bar Kalonikos, son of the sister of Titus, wished to become a proselyte. By means of necromancy he conjured up Titus. ' Who is most esteemed in the other world?' Titus replied, Israel, but warned him against embracing their faith, because of the great difficulty in fulfilling all its multitudinous commandments, and advised him to persecute them, for every one who oppresses Israel shall become a chief, as it is written: " Her adversaries are the chief " (Lament. I. 5) *i. e.*, whoever oppresses Israel will be a chief. He then inquired of Titus concerning his punishment in the other world! He rejoined, 'I suffered the penalty, I have asked for. Daily my ashes are collected, out of which my person is made, and burned again, and then my ashes are scattered over seven seas.' Balaam, whom he brought up next, also told him that the Jews were the most distinguished in the other world, and yet admonished him, "neither to seek their peace, nor their prosperity all his days forever," (Deut. xxiii. 6). What is your punishment in the other world? Balaam replied, ' I am boiled daily *in semine coitus.*' [1] At last he brought up Jesus, [2] of whom he asked the same question and from whom he received the same answer. He then asked : ' Shall I become a Jew?' to which the reply was : 'Seek their good and not their evil.' Whoever toucheth them, toucheth the apple of his eye. What is your punishment? He saith, ' In the boiling filth.' For Mar saith, ' Whoever mocketh at the words of the wise, is judged in the boiling filth.' "

In the Treatise *Sanhedrin* fol. 43, col. 1, at the bottom we read in non-expurgated editions : [On the eve of the Passover Jesus was hung. The herald, however, announced 40 days before : Jesus is led forth to be killed because he was a sorcerer and has misled Israel ; if any one knows something in his favor, let him come and say so. But as there

---

1. Pusey, *What is of Faith as to Everlasting Punishment* (London, 1880), p. 163, has not translated the words which we put into Latin, because as he says: " Decency again forbids to translate the answer put into the mouth of Balaam."

2. In the present editions we read for "Jesus," "Impious Israelite." The latter reading Wünsche rejects.

was nothing found in his favor, he was hung on the eve of the Passover. Ulla said: But was he worthy of favor, since he was a seducer, and the Scripture says: "Neither shalt thou spare, neither shalt thou conceal him," (Deut. xiii. 8). But it was different with Jesus, he was of royal descent. The rabbis have handed down that Jesus had five disciples: Matthew, Nikaeus, Nezer, Boni and Thoda. They brought Matthew [to suffer the extreme penalty of the law]. He said to them: Shall Matthew be destroyed? It is written: when (mathai) shall I appear before God? (Ps. xlii., 2). They said to him: Verily, Matthew shall be destroyed. It is written: When (mathai) shall he die and his name perish? (Ps. xli. 5). They brought Nikaeus. He said to them: Shall Nikaeus be destroyed? It is written: The innocent (naki) and righteous slay thou not (Exod. xxiii. 7.) They said to him: Verily Nikaeus shall be destroyed, for it is written: In the secret places does he murder the innocent (naki, Ps. x. 8). They brought Nezer. He said to them: Shall Nezer be destroyed? It is written: A branch (nezer) shall grow out of his root (Isa. xi. 1). They said to him: Verily, Nezer shall be destroyed, for it is written: "Thou art cast out of thy grave as an abominable branch (nezer, Isa. xiv. 19). They brought Boni. He said to them: Shall Boni be destroyed? It is written: Israel is my son (beni), even my first-born (Exod. iv. 22). They said to him: Verily Boni shall be destroyed. It is written: I will slay thy son (bincha), even thy first-born (Exod. iv. 23). They brought Thoda [Thaddeus?]. He said to them, Shall Thoda be destroyed? It is written: A psalm of Thoda (A. V., A psalm of praise, Ps. c., superscription). They said to him:

Verily, Thoda shall be destroyed, for it is written : whoso killeth Thoda glorificth me. (A. V., " Whoso offereth praise glorificth me," Ps. i. 23.)¹ " Neither shall any plague come nigh thy dwelling,' (Ps. xci. 10), means that thou have neither a son nor a pupil who allows his food to be burnt openly *i. e.*, who becomes an apostate [as for instance Jesus the Nazarene]. Tr. *Sanhedrin* fol. 103, col. 1.

2. STADA and PANDERA.² In treatise *Shabbath* fol. 104, col. 2, we read : Rabbi Eliezer said to the sages, Did not the son of Stada bring sorcery from Egypt in a cut of his flesh? They replied, he was a fool, and fools cannot be used in evidence. [You call him a son of Stada? he was a son of Panthera. Rav Chisda said : the husband of Mary was Stada, but her gallant was Pandera. But her husband was Papos ben Jehuda ! Yes, but his mother was Stada. But how, was not his mother Mary, the hair-dresser ! But (by Stada the mother of Jesus is meant indeed, which name was only her surname), as they used to say in Pumbaditha : she left her husband].³

---

1. This passage is one of the many curious examples of the way in which the Holy Scriptures are applied by the rabbis, or in the words of D. Moore (art. *Talmud* in Schaff-Herzog's Encyclop). " It is one of the strangest specimens of transparent fiction, and of silly trifling with the words of Scripture."

2. That Panthera was said to have been illegitimately the father of Jesus, was a tradition current before the composition of the Talmud ; for, as early as the second century, Celsus, against whom Origen wrote his treatise, introduced a Jew, who in speaking of the mother of Jesus, says that " when she was pregnant, she was turned out of doors by the carpenter to whom she had been betrothed, as guilty of adultery, and that she bore a child to a certain soldier named Panthera." The word " Panthera," or, as it is written in the Talmud *Pandera*, seems to have been used in an allegorical sense, meaning " the son of a wanton," for, according to allegorical exegesis, the *father* derives its name from τὸ πανθήρον, thus signifying " the personification of sensuality.'

3. We have followed the reading as given by Levy in his Lexicon s.v. *Stada*.—That Jesus wrought miracles was a well-known fact to his enemies, the Scribes and Pharisees, and to acknowledge which was to acknowledge His Messiahship. Hence they ascribed this, His power, to Satanic influences,—the very same thing which we find in the Talmud, where the miracles of Jesus are said to have

In *Sanhedrin* fol. 67, col. 1, we read : [thus they did with the son of Stada at Lydda [*i.e.*, they hid witnesses who could listen to his heresy without being seen] and hung him on the 'eve of the Passover. You call him a son of Stada, etc., as above]. [1]

3. BALAAM. In treatise *Sanhedrin* fol. 106, col. 2, where a Jewish Christian asks R. Chanina concerning the age of Balaam. The latter replied that nothing is written concerningly. Since, however, it is written that " bloody and deceitful men shall not live out half their days " (Ps. lv. 23), he was 33 or 34 years old. You are right, replied the Christian. I have seen myself a chronicle of Balaam, wherein it is written : 33 years old was Balaam, the lame, when he was killed by Phinehas, the robber.—The Jewish lexicographer, Levy (*Talmud, Lexicon* I., p. 236), remarks : Often Jesus is hidden under the name of Balaam. According to Jewish tradition Jesus was lame, because he was deprived of his magic virtue. And the Jewish historian Jost (*Geschichte des Judenthums* I. 405) refers to a remark of his friend Dr. Beer, who thinks that what is said concerning Balaam's age [33 years], no doubt refers to the death of Christ, and he finds this supposition the more probable since the murderer of Balaam, the robber Phinehas [Pinchas Listai], is mentioned, which name he thinks is nothing but a distortion for Pontius Pilate.

II. BIRTH AT BETHLEHEM ; POVERTY AND FLIGHT INTO EGYPT.

Reminiscences of the birth of Jesus at

---

been performed by means of sorcery. But this very assertion is an indirect testimony out of the mouths of the enemies of Jesus for the authenticity of His miracles.

1. We have here a direct testimony that Jesus was innocently slain.

Bethlehem, poverty and flight into Egypt, are given in the Jerusalem Talmud *Berachoth* fol. 5, col. 1 (and a little different in the *Midrash on Lamentations* I., 16) as follows : Rabbi Judan narrates : Whilst once a Jew was ploughing in his field, his ox was bellowing. An Arab passing, and hearing the ox bellow, said, Son of a Jew, Son of a Jew, loose thy oxen, and loose thy ploughs, for the Temple is laid waste. The ox bellowed a second time. The Arab said to him, Son of a Jew, Son of a Jew, yoke thy oxen and fit thy ploughs, for King Messiah has just been born. But, said the Jew, what is his name ? Menachem, said he. And what is the name of his father? Hezekiah (*i. e.*, power of God, strength of God), [1] said the Arab. To whom the Jew, But whence is he ? The other answered, from the palace of the King of Bethlehem-Judah. Away he went, and sold his oxen and his ploughs, and became a seller of infants' swaddling clothes. And he went about from town to town till he came to that place. There all the women bought of him, but the mother of Menachem bought nothing. He heard the voice of the women saying, O thou mother of Menachem, thou mother of Menachem, come and buy bargains for thy son. But she replied, I would rather strangle the enemy of Israel [the child], because on the day that he was born the Temple was laid waste. To whom he said, But we trust that, as it was laid waste at his feet, so at his feet it is being built again. [2] She said, I have no money. To whom he replied, What matters it ? Buy bargains for him, and if you have no money to-day, after

1 Reference to the supernatural birth of the Messiah.
2. " Behold, this child is set for the fall and rising against of many in Israel, and for a sign which shall be spoken against, Luke ii. 34."

some days I will come back and receive it.
After some days he returned to that place,
and said to her, How is the child doing?
And she said, After the time you saw me
last, winds and tempests came and snatched
him away from me. [1]

That the wise men had offered presents
was also known to the Talmudists : but
strange to say, they refer this to a Messiah
who is to come. Thus we read Tr. *Pesachim*
fol. 118, col. 2 : " In the future all nations
shall offer presents to King Messiah." Egypt
comes first, and do you think that he will
not receive their presents ? God says to
Messiah : " Accept them, for they have hos-
pitably received my children in Egypt [as is
said Ps. lxviii. 3] : Princes shall come out of
Egypt." Ethiopia thought : if He [Messiah]
accepted presents from the Egyptians, who
ill-treated the Israelites, how much more will
He receive them from us, who did not treat
them thus. The Holy One, blessed be He,
said to Him : Accept them, and " Ethiopia
shall soon stretch out her hands unto God."
Then came the Ishmaelites and said : " When
He accepted presents from those who were
not related with them, how much more will
He receive them from us, their brethren." [2]

III. SAYINGS OF JESUS.

It is a well-known fact that in the writings
of the early church fathers, a number of sayings of Christ are extant, which are not found
in the Gospels.[3] Two very interesting

---

1. This sudden disappearance refers no doubt to the flight into
Egypt.
2. What is strange in this narrative, which is also found in the
Midrash on Exodus xxvi. 15, is the fact that the Kings of *three
kingdoms, Egypt, Ethiopia, and of Ishmael,* are mentioned.
3. Comp. my *Life of Jesus according to Extra-Canonical
Sources* (New York, 1887), p. 124, *seq.*

passages, which are now no more extant in
the Gospels, are found in the Talmud as
follows:

Imma Salome was the wife of Rabbi
Eliezer and the sister of Rabban Gamaliel.
There was, in the neighborhood, a Jewish
Christian, who had the name that he would
not take a bribe. They wished to have a
laugh at him. So she brought him a golden
lamp, and they went before him. She said: I
wish that they should apportion unto me of
the property of the family. He [the Christian]
said to them: Apportion it. [He Gamaliel]
said: We have it written, "where there is a
son, a daughter does not inherit." He [the
judge] answered him: From the day that
ye were driven from your land the law of
Moses was taken away, and another law [or
rather "the gospel" as in old editions and
MSS.] given, in which it is written: the son
and daughter shall inherit alike. Next day,
he [Gamaliel] brought him a Libyan donkey.
He [the judge] said to them: I have looked
further on in the book; and it is written in it:
"I am not come to take from the law of
Moses, nor to add to the law of Moses am I
come." She said to him: "Let thy light
shine like the lamp." Rabban Gamaliel
said: The ass has come and trodden out the
lamp. Thus far the story (in Tr. *Shabbath* fol.
116, col. 1 and 2). The question arises: was
the passage—"the son and the daughter shall
inherit alike," in the Gospels or not? That
it was there cannot be questioned, since
the other passage agrees in essentials with
Matt. v. 17: "Think not that I came to
destroy the law or the prophets; I came not
to destroy, but to fulfil." From this it
would seem that the passage belonged to the
Gospel of St. Matthew, which, however, cannot now be decided. It may be that the cita-

---

tions here are from one of the recensions of the Gospels current at the time, and the probability is that it was the Gospel of Matthew, as we shall see further on.

Another story runs thus: Rabbi Eliezer (the same as above) was seized on the charge of being a Christian. The judge said to him: Thou, an aged man, busy thyself with such idle matters! He replied: I admit the faithful reproof of the judge. The latter, thinking that he referred to him, whereas he really meant God—said: Since you trust me you are discharged. He went home deeply distressed, and would receive no consolation from his disciples. Rabbi! cried Aqiba, allow me to say something, which I have learned from thee. Say it, was the reply. Hast thou not had a dispute with a Christian, and by approving what he said, got thyself into trouble? Aqiba! said he, thou just remindest me of a certain incident. Once upon a time I was walking in the upper street of Zipporith, when I met one [of the disciples of Jesus of Nazareth] whose name was James, of Kepher-Sachnia.[1] He said to me: " It is written in your law thou shalt not bring the hire of a whore into the house of the Lord thy God" (Deut. xxiii. 18). May a water-closet be made with it for the high-priest? This question I could not answer. Whereupon he said to me: Jesus [of Nazareth] taught me thus on the subject. It is written, She gathered it of the hire of an harlot, and it shall return to the hire of an harlot (Micah I. 7); that is, it came from an impure source, and it may be applied to an impure use. When I heard this explanation, I was pleased with it (Tr. *Aboda Zara* fol. 17, col. 1 and 2).

---

1. The Jewish historian Grätz, in his *Gnosticism and Judaism*, p. 25, note 22, identifies him with the Apostle James.

IV. HEALING IN THE NAME OF JESUS.

That the apostles healed in the name of Jesus, we know from the New Testament. The Talmud, too, bears testimony to this effect. Rabbi Eliezer ben Dama, a nephew of Rabbi Ishmael, having been bitten by a serpent, James, of Kepher-Sachnia, came to heal him [in the name of Jesus Pandera]. But Rabbi Ishmael would not permit this to be done. The sick asked the uncle to allow it, as he was ready to prove from the Scripture that it was permitted. But before he could produce his argument, the sick man died. "Happy Ben Dama!" said his uncle, "thou hast died in purity, without violating a precept of the wise."—Talm. Jerusalem *Shabbath* xiv. (toward the end), fol, 1, col. 4. This much is clear, that the apostle was known to have the power of healing in the name of Jesus.

PART III.

THE TALMUD AND THE GOSPELS.

THE Talmud has been used in the illustration of the New Testament, by Lightfoot, Schöttgen, Meuschen, Wettstein, Gfrörer, Robertson, Nork, Delitzsch, Wünsche. But in this department, also, its utility has been overestimated, and by none more than by Lightfoot himself, who says, in the dedication prefixed to his Talmudical exercitations, "Christians, by their skill and industry, may render them [the Talmudic writings] most usefully serviceable to their students and most eminently tending to the interpretations of the New Testament." But not so Isaac Vossius, who said Lightfoot would have

sinned less by illustrating the Evangelists from
the Koran than these *nebulæ rabbinicæ*, and
exclaimed: "Sit modus ineptiendi et cessent
tandem aliquando miseri Christiani Judaicis
istiusmodi fidere fabellis!" [*i. e.*, let Christians at length cease from playing the fool
and trusting to such wretched Jewish fables
as those contained in the Talmud]. The mistake of Lightfoot is repeated by Wünsche, [1]
whose *modus illustrandi et interpretandi* is like
a Jew writing an apology for Judaism.

There are some who accept the statement
of the late Mr. Deutsch for granted who said
"We need not urge the priority of the
Talmud to the New Testament. To assume
that the Talmud has borrowed from the New
Testament would be like assuming that
Sanscrit sprang from Latin, or that French
was developed from the Norman words found
in English." [2]   The same idea is expressed by
Rénan [3] when he says: "It is sometimes
supposed that, the compilation of the Talmud
being posterior to that of the Gospels, appro-
priations might have been made by the Jewish
compilers from the Christian morality. But
that is inadmissible; there was a wall of
separation between the Church and the
synagogue." But this wall of separation as
has been seen above, was not so high as to
preclude all and every intercourse, and the
notion that Christianity borrowed from the
Talmud is now given up. Says Dr. Geikie:
"There has been of late a tendency to exalt
the Talmud at the expense of the New
Testament, but let any one take up a translation of any part of it, and the exaggeration
of such an estimate will at once be seen." [4]

1. *Neue Beiträge zur Erläuterung der Evangelien*, Göttingen, 1878.
2. *The Talmud* in *Quarterly Review*, October, 1878.
3. *Life of Jesus*, p. 108.
4. *Life and Words of Christ* (New York, 1881) ii. 618.

Another writer says: "It is admitted, too, that the Talmud has borrowed from the neighbors of the Babylonian Jews superstitious views, and practices notoriously contrary to the spirit of Judaism. Why, then, may it not have appropriated Christian sentiments also?"[1] And a third writer[2] says:

"Though the oral traditions of the Mishna and portions of the Gemara were some of them doubtless antecedent to • the time of Christ by many generations, yet it cannot be proved in a single instance where there is identity of sentiment between the Talmud and the New Testament, that the Talmud did not borrow from the New Testament rather than the New Testament from the Talmud. It is not likely that an utterance as clear, condensed, and cutting as the Sermon on the Mount, as given by the Evangelists, was passed over with inattention by the learned senate of Jewish Rabbins. These teachings passed into the community, and became an animating and forming force in society; and they must, in the very nature of the case, have acted powerfully on all the existing schools of ethical and intellectual science. We find in Christ's discourses frequent allusions to the teachings of these men, searching reviews and criticisms of their doctrines. Much of the Sermon on the Mount is a statement of the errors in their teaching and the establishment of a higher code of morals. ' Ye have heard that it hath been said by them of old time, etc,; but *I* say unto you,' is, as we all know, a frequent form of summary in that discourse."

What has been asserted by different writers, we shall now prove by the following parallels from the Talmud to the Sayings of Jesus, giving at the same time the name of the author who uttered the sentence, and the time in which he lived. The date of the author must settle the question as to the priority once for all.

Matt. v. 3 :
" Blessed are the poor in spirit."

Sanhedrin fol. 43, col. 2: Rabbi Joshua ben Levi (A.D. 219-279) said, Behold, how acceptable before the Lord are the humble. While the temple stood, meat-offerings and sacrifices were offered in expiation for sins committed, but an humble spirit, such a one as immolates the desires of the flesh

---

1. D. Moore, art. *Talmud* in Schaff-Herzog's Encycl.
2. *Atlantic Monthly* (June, 1868).

and the inclination of the heart on the altar of his duty to his God, is acceptable in place of sacrifices, as the psalmist says (li. 19): " The sacrifices of God are a broken spirit."

Matt. v. 7:
" Blessed are the merciful, for they shall obtain mercy."

Shabbath fol. 151, col. 2: Rabban Gamaliel (A.D. 90–110) said : He who is merciful towards his fellow-creatures, shall receive mercy from heaven above.

Matt. v. 10:
" Blessed are they which are persecuted for righteousness' sake," etc.

Baba Kamma fol. 93, col. 1 : Rabbi Abahu (A. D. 279–320) said : Be rather one of the persecuted, than of the persecutors.

Matt. v. 19:
" Whosoever, therefore shall break one of these least commandments," etc.

Pirke Aboth 11. 1: Rabbi (A. D. 190) said : Be equally attentive to the light and to the weighty commandment.

Matt. v. 22:
" But I say unto you, that whosoever is angry with his brother," etc.

Sanhedrin fol. 58, col. 2 : Resh Lakesh (A. D. 219–280) said : Whosoever lifts up his hand against his neighbor, though he do not strike him, is called an offender and sinner.

Yomah ch. viii., a : Rabbi Eleazar ben Azariah (A. D. 82) said : the transgression which a man commits against God, the day of atonement expiates; but the transgression which he commits against his neighbor, it does not expiate, unless he has satisfied his neighbor.

Matt. v. 24:
" Leave thy gift before the altar, and go thy way; first be reconciled," etc.

Matt. v. 28:
" But I say unto you, that whosoever looketh on a woman to lust after her, committeth adultery," etc.

Berachoth fol. 24, col. 1 : Rabbi Shesheth (A. D. 285) says : Whosoever looketh on the little finger of a woman with a lustful eye is considered as having committed adultery.

Matt. v. 37:
" But let your communication, be Yea, Yea: Nay, Nay."

Baba Metzia fol. 49, col. 1 : Rabbi José berabbi Jehudah (A. D. 100–170) explains : What is the meaning of (Lev. xix. 36) : Just balances, just weights, a just ephah, and a just hin, since a hin was included in the ephah. To teach that your Yea be Yea, and your Nay be just. Abaye says this means that one should not say one thing with the mouth and another with the heart.

Matt. v. 40:
" And take away

Baba Kamma fol. 92, col. 2 : Rabba (A. D. 320–363) said to Rabba the son

thy coat let him have thy cloak also."

Matt. v. 44 : " Bless them that curse you."

Matt. vi. 1 : " Take heed that ye do not your alms before men to be seen of them."

Matt. vi. 9 : " Our Father which art in heaven."

Matt. vi. 19–21 : " Lay not up for yourselves treasures upon earth, where moth and rust doth corrupt, and where thieves break through and steal ; but lay up for yourselves treasures in heaven," etc.

of Mar, How is that popular saying ? If any one ask for thy ass, give him the saddle also.

Sanhedrin fol. 48, col. 2 : 49, col. 1 : Rabbi Jehudah (A. D. 120) said : Be rather of the accursed than of those that curse.

Chagiga fol. 5, col. 1 : Rabbi Yanaī (A. D. 120) said to a man who gave alms in such a public manner : You had better not give him anything : in the way you gave it to him you must have hurt his feelings.

This expression, which is found twice in the Mishna (*Yoma* viii. 9, and *Sotah* ix. 15), is certainly taken from the New Testament since the two rabbis who use this phrase lived after the destruction of the temple. Gfrörer, says Geikie (*l. c.* 11 p. 619), who took special pains to search for the Lord's Prayer in the Talmud, found that it could not be traced in any measure to older Jewish sources. Edersheim (*Life and Times of Jesus* I. 536) says : " It would be folly to deny that the Lord's Prayer, in its sublime spirit, tendency, combination and succession of petitions, is unique ; and that such expressions in it as 'Our Father,' 'the kingdom,' 'forgiveness,' 'temptation,' and others, represent in Rabbinism something entirely different from that which our Lord had in view."

Jerus Peah I. 3, we read Monebazus, the friend of Izates, Prince of Adiabene on the Tigris, a convert, with his prince to Judaism, about the time of the death of Christ, figures largely in the Talmud. After wild exaggeration of his wealth, the narrative goes on to say that his brothers and friends came to him and said, " Thy fathers gathered treasures and added to the treasures of their fathers, but thou scatterest them." He answered them, " My fathers had their treasures below, and I lay them up above, my fathers had their treasures where the hands (of men) may lay hold of them, I, where no hand can do so. My father's treasures yield no fruit, but I collect what gives fruit. My fathers stored away mammon, I, treasures of the soul : my fathers did it for others, I for myself. My fathers gathered them for the world, I, for the world to come."

Matt. vi. 26: "Behold the fowls of the air, for they sow not, neither do they reap," etc.	*Kiddushin* fol. 82, col. 2: Rabbi Simon ben Eleazar (3d century) said: Hast thou ever seen a beast or a bird that followed a trade, "and yet they are fed without toil. But these were only created to minister to me, while I was created to minister to my Maker. Was it not right, then, that I should be supported without toil? But I have marred my work and forfeited my support." [1]
Matt. vi. 31–34: "Therefore take no thought, saying, What shall we eat? or what shall we drink?" etc.	*Sota* fol. 48, col. 2: Rabbi Eliezer (of whom we have spoken already before, and who had intercourse with the apostle James) saith: He who hath still bread in his basket and saith what shall I eat to-morrow, belongeth to those of little faith.
Matt. vii. 2: "For with what judgment ye judge, ye shall be judged."	*Shabbath* fol. 127, col. 2: The post Mishnaic teachers said: he that judges his neighbor charitably, is himself judged charitably.
Matt. vii. 2: "With what mea-	*Sanhedrin* fol. 100, col. 1.: Rabbi Meïr (2d. cent.) said: With what

1. Prof. Delitzsch in his *Jüdisches Handwerkerleben* (Engl. transl. by Pick, *Jewish Artisan Life*, New York, 1883) quotes this passage in the following connection. We quote from our translation p. 23, *seq.*: "A learned Jew, Emmanuel Deutsch, of the British Museum, published in 1867 in the *Quarterly Review*, an article on the Talmud, in which he endeavored to show that between Judaism and Christianity no such wide difference exists as is generally believed since most of the pithy sayings and parables of the New Testament are not to be regarded as the original property of Christianity. The impression produced by this essay was all the deeper, the less able most of the readers were to compare the New Testament with this its glorification. . . . It would be very easy to demonstrate that the author has no idea of the essence of Christianity. . . . that the records of Christianity are so much older than their Talmudic parallels." After quoting the passage quoted above from the Talmud together with Matt. vi. 26, Prof. Delitzsch goes on: "Herr Deutsch draws many such parallels, avoiding with proud air the question of priority, as if it could not be raised at all. For when did this Simon live? He lived in the time of Emperor Adrian, full nigh a century later than Jesus. We will not, of course, insist on that account that he had drawn his maxim either direct from the gospel of St. Matthew, which was current in the Hebrew language, or indirectly from Christian lips; but if there is such a real coincidence, it is evident here, as in almost any other case, that the saying of Jesus is the original and that of Simon the copy. We say in *almost* any other case, but we might just as well say in *all* cases; for with the exception of Hillel, all Talmudical teachers whose maxims correspond to the words of the New Testament are of a far later date than Jesus and the records of Christianity."

sure ye mete it shall be measured to you again."

Matt. vii. 4: "Let me pull out the mote out of thine eye."

Matt. vii. 5: "Thou hypocrite, first cast out the beam out of thine own eye, and then shalt thou see," etc.

Matt. vii. 12: "Therefore all things whatsoever ye would that men should do to you, do ye even so to them; for this is the law and the prophets."

measure man metes it shall be measured to him from heaven.

Baba Bathra fol. 15, col. 2: Rabbi Johanan (A.D. 199–279) surnamed Bar Napha said: Do they say, Take the splinter out of thine eye, he will answer: Remove the beam out of thine own eye.

Arachin fol. 16, col. 2: Rabbi Tarphon (A.D. 120) says:

It would greatly astonish me if there could be found any one in this age who would receive an admonition. If he be admonished to take the splinter out of his eye, he would answer: Take the beam out of thine own.

Baba Metzia fol. 107, col. 2: *Baba Bathra* fol. 60, col. 2. Resh Lakesh (A.D. 275) said, What is the meaning of the passage, Examine thyself and search? (Zeph. ii. 11). He who will reprove others must himself be pure and spotless.

Shabbath fol. 3, col. 1: What is hateful to thyself, thou shalt not do to thy neighbor. This is the whole law, and the rest is commentary.

This is the much praised answer attributed to Hillel, and which induced writers like Rénan, Geiger, Deutsch, and the like to make Jesus an imitator of Hillel. But aside from the consideration, that Hillel cannot be claimed as the original author of this saying,[1] we must bear in mind the wide interval between the merely negative rule of the Jewish president, and the positive precept of the divine master. As to the saying itself, it existed long before Hillel's time, "and the

---

1. Jost. (*Gesch. d. Judenthums u. s. Sekten* I. p. 259) says, that the sentence which Hillel uttered, was one which was already known to everybody, and Farrar (*History of Interpretation* p. 50) thinks it possible that the later Rabbis in attributing this saying to Hillel were lighting their torches at the sun which yet they cursed.

9

fact that he in particular used it, accordingly
loses much of its significance, and any superstructure based upon the assumption that he
invented it falls to the ground."[1] Thus *Diogenes Laertius* relates that Aristotle (died
after 322 B.C.) being asked how we ought to
conduct ourselves towards our friends answered : " As we would wish they would
carry themselves toward us." And *Isocrates*,
who lived 400 years before the publication
of the gospel, said : ἃ πάσχοντες ὑφ ἑτέρων ὀργίσεσθε
ταῦτα τοῖς ἄλλοις μὴ ποιεῖτε, (*i. e.* " we must not do to
others that which would cause anger if.it
were done to ourselves.") In his *Ad. Demo-
nic.* c. 4, he says : " Be such towards your
parents as thou shalt pray thy children shall
be towards thyself ;" and the same, *In
Aeginet.* c. 23 : " That you would be such
judges to me as you would desire to obtain
for yourselves." Even among the sayings
of Confucius, the golden rule of the Saviour,
which Locke designates as the foundation of
all social virtue, this maxim is found in the
negative form : " What you do not wish
done to yourselves, do not to others ;" or,
as in the *Conversations* (book xv. c. 23)
where it appears condensed like a telegram :
ki su pok ük uk sü ü ing, i. e., "Self what not
wish, not do to man." In the apocryphal
book of Tobit we read (ch. iv. 15) : ὃ μισεῖς,
μηδενὶ ποιήσῃς (*i. e.* "do that to no man which
thou hatest ")[2] and in Ecclus. xxxi. 15, we
read : νόει τὰ τοῦ πλησίον καὶ ἐπὶ πράγματι διανοοῦ (*i. e.,*
" Judge of the disposition of thy neighbor
by thyself.")

---

1. Taylor, *The Teaching of the Twelve Apostles* (Cambridge, 1886),
p. 11.
     2. It is surprising that such an able scholar as Dr. Bacher (*Die
Agada der Tanaiten*, Strassburg, 1884) should write : As is known,
the book of Tobit perused the sentence of Hillel (" bekanntlich be-
nutzt auch das Buch Tobit den Satz Hillels. ") p. 7.

Pirke Aboth iii. 17 : Rabbi Eliezer ben Azariah (about A.D. 82) said: He whose knowledge surpasses his good deeds may be compared to a tree with many branches and a scanty root—every wind shakes and uproots it. But he whose good deeds excel his knowledge may be compared to a tree with a few branches and strong roots : if all the hurricanes of the world should come and storm against it, they would not move it from its place.

Aboth di Rabba Nathan, ch. **xxiv.** : Elisha ben-Abuyah (about A.D. 138) said: A man who studies the law, and acts in accordance with its commandments, is likened unto a man who builds a house the foundation of which is made of freestone, and the superstructure of bricks. Storm and flood cannot injure the house. But he who studies the law, but is destitute of good actions, is likened unto the man who builds the foundation of his house of brick and mortar and raises the upper stories with solid stone. The flood will soon undermine and overturn the house.

Shabbath fol. 153, col. 1 : Rabbi Johanan ben Zacchai (fl. after the destruction of the Temple) said : It is like a king who invited his servants to a banquet, but did not appoint the time. The wise among them adorned themselves, and waited at the entrance of the King's palace, saying: can there be anything wanting at the King's house [which may delay the banquet] ? But the foolish among them went after their work, saying : can there be a banquet without preparation? Suddenly the king asked for his servants, when the wise among them entered adorned, but the foolish came into his presence soiled. The King rejoiced to meet the wise servants, but was angry with the foolish servants. Let those, said he, who have adorned themselves for the banquet sit down to eat and drink, but let those who have not adorned themselves for the banquet stand and look on.

Matt. vii., 24–27 : "Therefore whosoever heareth these sayings of mine, and doeth them, I will liken him unto a wise man which built his house upon a rock," etc.

Matt. xxv. 1–14 : PARABLE OF THE TEN VIRGINS.

Matt. ix, 37 : "The harvest truly is plenteous, but the laborers are few," etc.	*Pirke Aboth* ii. 15 : Rabbi Tarphon (about A.D. 120) said, The day is short, and the task is great, and the workmen are sluggish, and the reward is great, and the Master of the house is urgent.
Matt. x. 8: "Freely ye have received, freely give."	*Nedarim* fol. 47, col. 1 : Samuel (d. A.D. 257): Behold I have taught you statutes and judgments, even as the Lord my God commanded me (Deut iv. 5). As I have taught you freely, so teach you freely.
Matt. xxiii. 12 : "and whosoever shall exalt himself shall be abased ; and he that shall humble himself shall be exalted."	*Baba Metziah* fol. 85, col. 2 : Rabbi Jeremiah (+ A.D. 250) said : Whoever makes himself little in this world, for the sake of the words of the Law will be made great in the world to come, and whoever makes himself like a slave in this world, for the sake of the words of the Law, will be made free in the world to come.
Mark ii. 27 : "The Sabbath was made for man, and not man for the Sabbath."	*Yoma* fol. 85, col. 2. Rabbi Jonathan ben Joseph (fl. after the destruction of the temple) says : it is written : Ye shall keep the Sabbath therefore, for it is holy unto you (Exod. xxxi., 14). It is delivered into your power, not you into its.

Without increasing parallels, it will be evident that the claim that the New Testament copied the Talmud must accordingly be stigmatized, once for all, as a vain glorification of modern Judaism, which, on the one hand rejects the Talmud as a religious code, but, on the other, makes use of it for controversial purposes.

THE TALMUD'S TESTIMONY CONCERNING THE CHRISTIANS AND CHRISTIANITY.

It is now admitted by Jewish writers that the word *min* (pl. *minim*), [1] so often men-

---

1. Out of fear for the censor the word *Sadduki* was substituted especially in the Babylonian Talmud. But after the destruction of the Temple the Sadducees disappeared entirely.

tioned in the Talmud, denotes the Christians, while *minuth* means Christianity.

1. STUDY OF THE SCRIPTURES BY THE
CHRISTIANS.—That the Christians studied the
Scriptures is best illustrated by the following : Rabbi Abahu recommended Rabbi
Saphra to the Christians as a good scholar.
Thereupon the Christians remitted him the
taxes for thirteen years. But it happened
that one day Rabbi Saphra was asked to
give an explanation of Amos iii. 2 : " 'You
only have I known of all the families of the
earth ; therefore I will punish you for all your
iniquities,' " adding, " How can you suppose
God to vent his wrath on one whom he
addresses as his friend ? " Rabbi Saphra
was unable to reply. The Christians then
took him, and tied a rope round his head,
and tormented him. When Rabbi Abahu
came and found him in this plight, he demanded of the Christians : " Why do you
torment this Rabbi so cruelly ? " They
replied, " Did you not tell us that he was a
very learned man? To the first question
we asked of him he was unable to make any
answer." " I did, indeed, say," answered
Rabbi Abahu, " that he was a good scholar
in the Talmud, but not in the Scriptures."
" But how is it that you understand the
Scriptures and he does not ? " To this Rabbi
Abahu answered : " We, who come in con-
tact with you Christians are obliged, for our
self-preservation, to study the Scriptures ;
because you dispute so often with us from
the Scriptures, and because we know that
you study them ; but the other Jews, who
live among Gentiles, have no need of that,
as they do not dispute with them concerning the Scriptures." [1]—What a gloomy pict-

---

1. *Aboda Zarah* fol. 4, col. 1.

ure! The Jews read the Bible, not because
they are concerned about the "one thing
needful," but only for the sake of controversy.   As another illustration of the acquaintance of the Christians with the Scriptures, we quote the following: " The disciples asked Rabbi Aqiba whether, in case
that the lot appointed the goat which
stood on the left of the priest, for a sacrifice
in the Temple, the position of the goats
should be changed? He replied: 'Give the
Christians no occasion for assailing us;'[1]
or, as Rashi explains it: 'To the disciples
of Jesus of Nazareth who discourse concerning the Scriptures, that they do not say you
(Jews) act arbitrarily.'"[2]

2. CIRCULATION OF THE GOSPELS.—That
the gospels and other writings of the
Christians were in circulation at an early
time, we see from the many enactments of
the Jewish rabbis against them. At the
time that the rules for keeping the Sabbath
were under consideration, it was asked in
the schools whether, if the gospels and
other books of the Christians should happen
to fall into the fire, it would be permissible
to rescue them from the fire, inasmuch as
the name of God was written in them, and
they contained numerous quotations from
the Old Testament. "The Gospels and the
other books of the Christians are not to be
rescued from the fire." Rabbi José said
that the names of God should, by all means,
be rescued, and the remainder thrown back
into the flames. Said Rabbi Tarphon: "By
the life of my son, should they come into
mine hands I will burn them together with
the names of God which they contained.

---

1. *Yoma* fol. 40, col. 2.
2. *L.c.* Venice Edition ; quoted by Goldfahn in Graetz' *Monats-schrift*, 1873, p. 109.

Were I pursued by a serpent, I would
rather take refuge in a temple of idols than
in the house of the Christians; for the latter
were wilful traitors, while the heathen
sinned in ignorance of the right way, and
concerning them the Scripture says: ' Behind the doors, also, and the posts, hast
thou set up thy remembrance.' (Isa. lvii.
8)."[1] Rabbi Ishmael said "The question
is not one which should give us any trouble
to answer. If, in order to make peace between two persons, the Law permitted the
complete effacement of a passage of Holy
Scripture in which the name of God has
been most solemnly invoked (Numb. v. 23),
why should we deal gingerly with the writings of these people, who are sowing hatred,
hostility and discord between Israel and his
Heavenly Father. And, as we do not rescue them from flames, so not from the sudden falling of a building, or from rushing
waters, or aught else that may accomplish
their ruin."[2] According to Rabbi Aqiba
those have no portion in the world to come
who read in outside books, *i. e.*, books of the
minim or Christians (as the text of the
Mishna is explained in the Gemara). [3]

Whatever may be the date assigned by
modern critics to the Gospel of Matthew,
certain it is that it circulated in some form
at a very early date, as will be seen from
the following: Gamaliel II. (died about the
year 110 A.D.) was asked: "How do you
know that the dead will rise again?" He

---

1 This his animosity against Christianity, induced some, as
Lightfoot, Carpzov, and others, to maintain that Rabbi Tarphon
is the same Typho who is the interlocutor in Justin Martyr's
Dialogue. Schürer (*Neutestamentliche Zeitgeschichte*, 2d ed. vol. ii.
p. 312) thinks this identity to be possible.
2. *Shabbath* fol. 116, col. 1. conf. Bacher, *Die Agada der Tannai-
ten* p. 266.
3. *Sanhedrin* fol. 100, col. 2.; conf. also Joël, *Blicke in die Re-
ligionsgeschichte zu Anfang des Zweiten Christlichen Jahrhun-
derts* (Breslau, 1880) p. 70 *seq.*

adduced passages in proof of the Resurrection from the Law (Deut. xxxi. 16), the
prophets (Isa. xxvi. 19), and the Hagiogra-
pha (Song of Songs, vii. 10. A.D. 9). These
passages were rejected as insufficient. He
finally quoted the words "the land which
the Lord sware unto your fathers to give
them" (Deut. xi. 21). Since the fathers
were dead, the promise must have promised
a resurrection, when alone the land could
be given to these fathers. [1]   This shows the
force of the interpretation given by Christ in
Matt. xxii. 32 ("I am the God of Abraham,
and the God of Isaac, and the God of Jacob!
God is not the God of the dead, but of the
living"), and the inference he deduced there-
from.

Another proof for the early existence of
Matthew's Gospel may be derived from a
quotation made by Eliezer (conf. Matt. vi.
30–34 above), Gamaliel's brother-in-law.

3. POWER AND INFLUENCE OF CHRIS-
TIANITY.—The power and influence of
Christianity is best attested by the Talmud
when we read: "It is different with Christianity; it attracts." [2]   In order to break its

---

1. *Sanhedrin* fol. 90, col. 2.
2. Talmud *Aboda Zarah* fol. 27, col. 2. As an illustration we
quote the following as related in the *Midrash on Ecclesiastes* 1. 8:
Rabbi Hanina, nephew of Rabbi Joshua, went to Capernaum; and
the Christians bewitched him, and made him ride into the town on
an ass upon the Sabbath. When he returned to his uncle, Rabbi
Joshua gave him an unguent which healed him from the bewitch-
ment. But Joshua said to him: "Since you have heard the bray-
ing of the ass of that wicked one, you can no longer remain on the
soil of Israel." Hanina went down to Babylon, and there died in
peace. Dr. Farrar, who quotes this story (*Expositor* vol. vi. 1877,
p. 423) says: The expression 'the ass of that wicked one' is only
too plainly and sadly an allusion to the ass ridden by our Lord in
his triumphal entry into Jerusalem; and the suppression of the
name of Jesus is in accordance with the practice of only mentioning Him in an oblique and cryptographic manner.—Lowe (*Frag-
ment of Talmud Babli*, Cambridge, 1879, p. 71) translated for
"ass" *wine*—in the Talmud both words have one expression—and
thinks that the Christians intoxicated him with the wine of their
agapai, which they seem to have celebrated on Friday night.
More probable, perhaps, is the meaning of Delitzsch, (*Ein Tag in
Capernaum*, p. 25, Leipsic, 1873) who says that the "ass of that
wicked" refers to the foolish preaching of the crucified.

influence and to check its growth, shortly before the destruction of Jerusalem, the first formal anathema was hurled by the entire Rabbinic assembly, which had met at Jamnia or Jabneh, under the auspices of Gamaliel II. Thus the great Rabbi Maimonides says: "In the days of Rabbi Gamaliel (the elder)¹ the minim increased in Israel, and afflicted Israel, and seduced men to turn away from God. Then when he saw that it was indispensably necessary, he instituted that imprecation in which God is besought that the minim should be destroyed, and added it to the eighteen prayers, so that the whole number now found in the Prayer Book is nineteen.² Thus far Maimonides. From the Talmud we learn the history of the prayer which is as follows: Simon Pakuli arranged the eighteen benedictions before Rabban Gamaliel in their present order at Jabneh. Said Rabban Gamaliel to the sages, "Is there none who knows to prepare a benediction against the Zadukim?" Then arose Samuel the Little and prepared it.³ This prayer, which now forms the twelfth of the so-called Shemone Esreh, or Eighteen Benedictions, reads now, "O let the slanderers have no hope; all the wicked be annihilated speedily and all the tyrants be cut off quickly, humble thou them quickly in our days. Blessed art thou, O, Lord! who destroyest enemies and humblest tyrants." We doubt very much that this was the original form of the prayer, because the following is also found: "Be thou not a hope to the meshumadim (apostates), but may the minim, the doubled-tongued,

---

1. It was not Gamaliel the elder (Conybeare and Howson, *Life and Epistles of St. Paul*, vol. 1, p. 70) but as is now generally held, his grandson, Gamaliel II., who sanctioned that prayer.
2. *Hilcoth Tephilla* c. 11. 3. *Berachoth* fol. 28, col. 2.

the infidels, the traitors perish together in a
moment; may the enemies of thy people
Israel be speedily annihilated; mayest thou
speedily destroy the Kingdom of Pride and
rend it in pieces; mayest thou humble them
speedily in these our days. Blessed art
thou, O, God, for thou shalt break into fragments the wicked, and humble the proud."[1]
Whatever the form of the so-called *Birkath
ha-minim*—as it is called—may have been,
its existence is attested by Epiphanius,[2] who
says that the Jews three times during the
day curse and excommunicate (the Naza-
renes.) The same we also learn from
Jerome [3] and Justin the Martyr.[4]

In spite of all stringent measures the number of believers increased. As many cher-
ished the Christian faith in secret, it was
enacted that in a case a reader erred in one
of the benedictions, he was not to be removed from the reading-desk, but in case he
erred in the benediction against the *minim*,
he was to be removed, because he was then
suspected of being a *min* himself.[5]

1. Quoted from Reichardt (*The Relation of the Jewish Christians to the Jews in the First and Second Centuries*, London, 1884,
p. 46.) who says that he copied it from an old manuscript.
2. *Advers Haeres* xxix. 9 (ed. Petav. p. 124): τρὶς τῆς ἡμέρας
ὅτε εὐρὰς ἐπιτέλουσιν ἑαυτοῖς ἐν ταῖς συναγωγαῖς ἐπαρῶνται
αὐτοῖς, καὶ ἀναθεματίζουσι τρὶς τῆς ἡμέρας φάσκοντες ὅτι
ἐπικατάρασι θεὸς τοὺς Ναζωραίους. With regard to these words
of Epiphanius, the Jewish historian Grätz (*Geschichte* iv. 434.)
remarks that Epiphanius, being by birth a Jew, is a competent
witness that this formula was directed against the Jewish Christians.
3. *Ad Jesajam* 5, 18-19 (ed. Vallarsi iv. 81: "(Judaei) usque
hodie perseverant in blasphemiis et ter per singulos dies in omni-
bus synagogis sub nomine Nazarenorum anathematizant vocabu-
lum Christianum." Comp. also ad Jesajam 49, 7 (ed. Vallarsi iv.
565): "(Judaei Christo) ter per singulos dies sub nomine Nazarenorum maledicunt in synagogis suis." And *Ad Jesajam* 52, 4 *seq.*
(ed. Vallarsi iv, 604): "(Judaei) diebus ac noctibus blasphemant Sal-
vatorem et sub nomine, ut saepe dixi, Nazarenorum ter in die in
Christianos congerunt maledicta.
4. *Dialog. cum. Tryph.* c. 16: καταρώμενοι ἐν ταῖς συναγωγαῖς
ὑμῶν τοὺς πιστεύοντας ἐπὶ τὸν Χριστόν.
5. *Berachoth* fol. 29, col. 1. We are told that a year after the
composition of the prayer against the *minim*, its very author

It was also enacted that none should be received as disciples or allowed to attend the public schools except those whose inner convictions were found, on examination, to harmonize fully with the outward observances which they sought to undertake.[1]

4. CUSTOMS AND USAGES.—The influence of Christianity being felt more and more, the Jews changed some of their ancient customs. Thus the "standing men"[2] used to fast on several days of the week, but not on Sunday. And why not upon a Sunday? Rabbi Samuel bar Nachmani says because it is the third day from the formation (of Adam).[3] Resh Lakesh says because of the additional soul given to man on Friday (for the increase of his appetite), and taken away again at the close of the Sabbath, as it is said (Exodus xxxi. 17): " He rested

---

while before the reading-desk, could no more remember it and from three to four hours he tried to recall it to his memory, yet without avail. He was, however, not removed. Had the author changed his mind with regard to those for whom his prayer was intended ? or did he himself belong to the church ? or was he already a member of the church when he composed this prayer *stante pede,* and composed it only in order to avert the suspicion of being a *min* himself ?

1. *Berachoth* fol. 28, col. 1.   The Jewish writer, M. Friedländer (*Patristische and Talmudische Studien,* p. 141) is inclined to think that Gamaliel introduced this measure in order to clear himself from the reproach as if he favored the new sect. This would prove that he was suspected of being in secret a Christian, as is stated Clementine *Recognitions* I., 65-66. The Jewish historian Grätz (*Geschichte der Juden* iv. p. 427) tells us that in a church at Pisa, the tomb of Gamaliel was shown with the following inscription :

"Hoc in Sarcophago requiescunt corpora sacra
　　Sanctorum . . . . Sanctus Gamaliel,
　　Gamaliel divi Pauli didascalus olim,
　　Doctor et excellens Israelita fuit
　　Concilii magni fideique per omnia cultor."

I am rather inclined to think that this enactment was made by Gamaliel II., at Jabneh, in order to keep away the many Christian believers.

2. " Standing men " has reference to those Israelites who were commissioned to act as delegates, representing the nation at the Temple, in Jerusalem ; and because they had to *stand* near the priest during the offering of the daily sacrifice, they were called " the standing men."

3. Adam was created on Friday ; Sunday was therefore the third day after his creation, and upon the third day man is supposed to be weak, for it is said (Genesis, xxxiv., 25), "and it came to pass on the third day when they were sore."

and was refreshed ;" *i. e.*, having rested,
alas! the additional soul is lost. [1]   It will be
seen that the reasons proffered by the
Talmud are not cogent.   The true reason,
however, is "because of the Christians"
(as the older editions of the Talmud read),
who, says Rashi, make their festival upon
that day.   The idea is, that those who fasted
had not to work, and a cessation from work
on Sunday might have the appearance of
observing the Christian Sunday *i. e.*, when
the Temple was still in existence.

We are also, told that it was proposed
that the Ten Commandments, which were
recited every morning in the Temple, should
be adopted in the synagogues throughout
the land ; but this was not carried into effect because of the troubles of the minim, [2]
because—as the Jerusalem Talmud explains [3] —it was feared that the Christians
would thus be induced to believe that they,
the Jews, were in a similar plight as themselves, and only pledged to the observance
of the Ten Commandments (*i. e.*, the moral
law). [4]   Another curious example of the
necessity which the Jews felt of protesting
against the Christians is the following : The
inhabitants of Jericho were in the habit of
repeating, each to himself, in a low voice,
the words : "Blessed be the name of the
glory of His Kingdom forever and ever"
after the words "Hear, O Israel, the Lord
our God is one Lord" (Deut. vi. 4), had
been recited aloud. But, says, Rabbi Ab-
bahu, it was enacted, that these words should
be repeated in a loud voice, on account of

1. *Taanith* fol. 27, col. 2.
2. *Berachoth* fol. 12, col. 1 ; *Taamid* fol. 32, col. 2.
3. *Berachoth* fol. 3, col. 3.
4. But this was probably not the true reason. The real ground
seems to have been to avoid conforming a part of the Jewish sere-
vice to the Christian, and thus making the joining of the churches
much easier.

the troubles occasioned by the minim,[1] but at Nehardea, where there are no minim, they repeat it to this day in a subdued voice.

Great care was taken that the prayers contained not the least sign of a Christian phraseology. Thus we read : A person who, in his prayer says, the Good bless thee, shows a Christian manner ; but if one says, " as thy mercies extend even to birds' nests, have mercy also upon us," he shall be silenced. [2] The words : The good bless thee, probably belonged to an ancient Christian liturgy, and the words, " as thy mercies extend even to birds' nests," reminded too much of Matt. x. 29, hence that person was silenced.

Even the dress of the person who acted as reader of the synagogue, was made a test. Thus we read : if a person should say, I will not minister at the reading desk in colored clothes, he may not be permitted to do so in white ones ; if he refuses to minister with sandals to his feet, he may not be permitted to minister barefooted.[3] To this Mishnaic injunction the Gemara remarks : The reason for this is because such a one might belong to the Christians. Rashi, in his commentary on that paragraph, remarks that the Christians used to have regard to such things.

And because the Christians used to pray eastwards, doubts were expressed as to the feasibility of having the face eastward during prayer, and in order to protest most emphatically against the increasing heresy (*i. e.* Christianity), it was recommended to turn the face westward during prayer.[4] From all this it is evident that the growth of the

---

1. *Pesachim* fol. 56, col. 1. Reference is here no doubt to the Trinity.
2. *Megillah* fol. 25, col. 1.   3. *Ibid.* fol. 24, col. 2.
4. *Baba Bathra*, fol. 25, col. 1, Löw, *Der Synagogale Ritus* (in Grätz's *Monatsschrift*, 1884), p. 313.

Christian Church must have been very rapid, otherwise the synagogue would not have required such measures which were intended to check the advancement of the gospel.

LITERATURE OF THE TALMUD.

I. EDITIONS. The first complete edition of the Babylonian Talmud was published by Bomberg (Venice, 1520–'23, 12 vols., fol). This formed the basis of later ones. Since that time editions have been published at different places, which are enumerated by R. N. Rabbinowicz in *Kritische Uebersicht der Gesammt und Einzelausgabe des Babylonischen Talmuds seit* 1484 (Munich, 1877, written in Hebrew). The most recent edition is that published at Wilna, 1880–1886, in 26 vols. All these editions are without the anti-Christian passages, which are still found in the Amsterdam edition of 1644.

II. TRANSLATIONS. The following parts have been translated into German:

1. *Berachoth* by Pinner (Berlin, 1842); 2. *Aboda Zara* by Ewald (Nuremberg, 1868); 3. *Taanith* by Straschun (Halle, 1883); 4. *Megilla* by Rawicz (Frankfort, 1883); 5 *Rosh-ha-Shanah* by the same (*Ibid.* 1886). The Haghadistic parts have been translated into German by A. Wünsche (Leipsic, 1886 –1887, 2 vols.).

III. TEXTUAL CRITICISM. Rabbinowicz, *Variae Lectiones in Mischnam et in Talmud Babylonicum quum ex aliis Libris Antiquissimis et Scriptis et Impressis tum e Codice Monacensi Praestantissimo collectae, Annotationibus instructae*, Munich, 1868, seq.

IV. LINGUISTIC HELPS. Buxtorf, *Lexicon Chaldaicum, Talmudicum et Rabbinicum* (Basil. 1640, fol.; new edition by B. Fischer, Leipsic, 1869–'75); Levy *Neu-*

hebräisches und Chaldäisches Wörterbuch, etc. (*Ibid.* 1875–1887, not yet completed) ; *Aruch* by Nathan ben Jechiel ; (new critical edition by A. Kohut, *Plenum Aruch Targum Talmudico Midrasch Verbale et Reale Lexicon* (Vienna, 1878, *seq.*). Rülf, *Zur Lautlehre der aramäisch-talmudischen Dialecte* (part I., *Die Kehllaute,* Leipsic, 1879) ; Berliner, *Beiträge zur hebräischen Grammatik in Talmud und Midrasch* (Berlin, 1879).

Since the Talmud is the great storehouse of all and everything, it has been treated in treatises, the number of which is legion and to enumerate which would be tedious. Very instructive, however, is *Einleitung in den Talmud* (a reprint of the art. *Talmud* in Herzog Real-Encycl. 2d ed.) by H. L. Strack, Leipsic, 1887.

INDEX.

A.

Abina, 72.
Abtalion, 17, 19.
Alexander, 97.
Amoraim, 68, 73.
Amulet, 80.
Antigonus of Socho, 15.
Aqiba, 37 *seq.* 122.
Aquinas, 31, 37.
Ashé, 71.
Astrology, 80.
Atlantic Monthly, 125.

B.

Babylonian Talmud, 71 *seq.*
Bacher, 130, 135.
Balaam, 118.
Bar Cochba, 40.
Bethera, sons of, 18.
Bloch, viii.
Bonaventura, 31.
Briggs, 43.
Buxtorf, 77.

C.

Carpzov, 135.
Charms, 81.
Christianity, power and influence of, 136 *seq.*
Christians study the Scriptures, 133 *seq.;* customs and usages of, 139; prayer against, 137 *seq.*
Clarke, 27.
Confucius, 130.
Conybeare and Howson, 137.
Cornhill Magazine, 27, 85.

D.

Da Costa, 92.
Delitzsch, 19, 74, 94, 128, 136.
Demons, 81.
Deutsch 27, 84, 94, 124, 128.
Diogenes Laertius, 130.
Disraeli, 90.

E.

Edersheim, 95, 128.
Edinburgh Review, 11, 84, 85, 90, 96.
Eliezer ben Hyrcanus, 36, 38, 122.
Epiphanius, 138.
Etheridge, 32, 98.
Ezra, 12.

F.

Farrar, 12, 13, 14, 40, 45, 84, 92, 39, 98, 111, 113, 129, 136.
Friedländer, 139.

G.

Gamaliel I., Rabban, vii., 31, 121.
"   II., 36.
Geiger, 19, 21.
Geikie, 95, 124, 127.
Gemara, 68, 69.
Gemarici. 68.
God, as presented in the Talmud, 79 *seq.*
Goldfahn, 134.
Gospels, and the Talmud, 123 *seq.;* circulation of, 134 *seq.*
Graetz, 32, 122, 138, 139.

H.

Heine, 27.
Herzfeld, 14.
Hillel, 18 *seq.;* no reformer 21, 130.
Hurwitz, 82, 94.

I.

Imma Salome, 121.
Ismael, 41, 42.
Isocrates, 130.

J.

James, the apostle, vi.
Jerome, 29, 138.
Jerusalem Talmud, 69 *seq.*
Jesus, the Talmud on, 113 *seq.;* disciples of, 116; birth, poverty and flight, 118–120; sayings of 120 *seq.;* healing in the name of, 123.
Jochanan ben Eliezer, 69.
Joël, 135.
Johanan ben Sakkai, 34 *seq.*
Jose ben Joëser, 16.
"   " Jochanan, 16.
"   the Galilean, 43.
Joseph ben Halafta, 44.
Josephus, 33.
Joshua ben Hananja, 37, 38.
"   " Perachia, 16, 113.
Jost, 25, 118, 129.

Juda ben Ilai, 44.
"   " Tabbai, 17.
" the Holy, 44 *seq.*
Justin Martyr, 138.

L.

Leslie, 88.
Levin, 88.
Levy, 14, 100, 118.
Lightfoot, 36, 75, 123, 135.
Löw, 141.
Lowe, 136.

M.

Meïr, 44.
Meklenburg, vi.
Messiah, Talmudic notices on, 99 *seq.*
Milman, v. 11. 92.
Mishna, 47 *seq.;* contents of, 48–64; editions of, 65; translations of, 65; helps to, 66 *seq.*
Moore, 117, 125.

N.

Nahum of Gimso, 37, 38.
Nathan, 44.
Nazarene, 113.
Nithai of Arbela, 66.

P.

Palestinian Talmud, 69.
Pandera, 117.
Panthera, 117.
Passages quoted or referred to:
Gen. xv. 13, p. 112.
    xlix. 10, p. 110.
Exod. iv. 22, p. 116.
      23, p. "
    xvi. 5, p. 22.
    xxiii. 7, p. 116.
Levit. xiii. 13, p. 102.
    xix. 36, p. 127.
Num. v. 23, p. 135.
Deut. vii. 25, p. 104.
    viii. 3, p. 112.
    xi. 21, p. 136.
    xiii. 8, p. 116.
    xxiii. 6, p. 115.
      18, p. 122.
    xxxii. 36, p. 102.
Ps.   x. 8, p. 116.
    xli. 5, p. "
    xlii. 2, p. "
    lv. 23, p. 118.
    lxviii. 3. p. 120.
    lxxii. 16, p. 79.
      17, p 110.
    xxx. 6, p. 104.
    xc. 4, p. 103.
      15, p. 112.
    xci. 7, p. 109.
      10, p. 117.
    xcii. 1, p. 103.
    xcv. 10, p. 111.
    civ. 26, p. 14.
Eccl. i. 9, p. vii.

Isa. i. 26, p. 107.
    ii. 11, p. 103.
    v. 7, p. 107.
    xiv. 19, p. 116.
    xviii. 5, p. 106.
    xxiii. 15, p. 111.
    xxx. 18, p. 105.
      15, p. 106.
    xlviii. 11, p. 108.
    xlix. 7, p. 106.
    liii. 4, p. 110.
    liv. 9, p. 112.
    lv. 3, p. 106.
    lvii. 8, p. 135.
    lix. 15, p. 101.
      16, p. 108.
      19, 20, p. 107.
    lx. 2, p. 111.
      21, p. 107.
    lxii. 5, p. 112.
    lxiii. 4, p. 112.
    lxiv. 3, p. 112.
Jer. iii. 14, p. 106.
      22, p. 105.
    iv. 1, p. 106.
    x. 2, p. 80.
    xvi. 13, p. 110.
    xxv. 30, p. 79.
    xxx. 9, p. 110.
      21, p. 110.
    xxxi. 8, p vii.
Lam. i. 5, p. 115.
      16, p. 110.
Ezek. xvii, 23, p. vii.
    xxix. 21, p. 107.
    xxxii, 14, p. 106.
    xxxvii. 25, p. 110.
Dan. vii. 17, p. 108.
    xii. 7, p. 106.
Hos. vi. 2, p. 103.
Am. iii. 2, p. 133.
    iv. 7, p. 100.
    v. 18, p. 110.
    ix. 11, p. 100.
Mic. i. 7, p. 122.
    v. 3, p. 109.
Hab. ii. 3, p. 104, 105.
Zeph. ii. 11, p. 129.
    iii. 11, p. 107.
    v. 12, p. 107.
Hag. ii. 5, p. 104.
Zech. ix. 9, p. 108, 111.
Mal. iii. 7, p. 106.
Ecclus. xxxi. 15, p. 130.
Tobit. iv. 15, p. 130.
Matt. v. 3, p. 125.
      7, p. 126.
      10, p. 126.
      17, p. 121.
      19, p. 126.
      22, p. 126.
      24, p. 126.
      28, p. 126.
      37, p. 127.
      40, p. 127.
      44, p. 127.
    vi. 1, p. 127.
      19–21, p. 128.
      26, p. 128.
      31–34, p. 128.

Passages referred to, continued :
Mat.vii. 2, p. 128.
    4, p. 129.
    5, p. 129.
    12, p. 129.
    24, p. 131.
    29, p. 14.
  ix. 37, p. 132.
  x. 8, p. 132.
    29, p. 141.
  xx. 30, 31, p. 100.
  xxii. 32, p. 136.
  xxiii. 12, p. 132.
Mark xv. 32, p. 100.
Luke ii. 34, p. 119.
Acts xv. 16, p. 100.
Paul and Gamaliel, vii.
Pinner, 43.
Pressensé, 16.
Pusey, 115.

R.

Rabbi, 44 *seq.*
Reichardt, 138.
Rénan, v. 19, p. 124.
Reynolds, 36.

S.

Sabbath made for man, 132.
Schaff, 96.
Schürer, 135.
Scribes, 12.
Scriptures studied by the Chris-
    tians, 133.
Shammai, 22, 28.
Shemaiah, 17, 19.
Simon ben Gamaliel, 33, 43.
  "   "   Jochai, 44.

Simon ben Shetach, 17.
  "   the Just, 12, 15.
Soferim, 12.
Stada, 117.
Stanley, 14, 15, 29, 30.
Stanton, v.
Sunday, 140.

T.

Talmud, Jerusalem. 69.
Talmud, Babylonian, 71 *seq.;*
    name, character, language, 72
    seq.; appendix to, 76 *seq.;* guide
    to the treatises of the, 78 ; liter-
    ary and moral character of,
    77–87 ; accusations against the,
    88 ; how to avoid them, 88 *seq.;*
    different opinions on the, 90–98 ;
    literary use of, 98 *seq.;* notices
    concerning the Messiah in the,
    99–112 ; names of Jesus in the,
    113 *seq.;* the gospels and the,
    123 *seq.;* testimony concerning
    the Christians and Christianity,
    132 *seq.;* literature on, 142 *seq.*
Tanaim, 15.
Tarphon, 43, 134.
Taylor, 130.

V.

Virgins, parable of the ten, 131.
Vossius, 123.

W.

Wachner, 74.
Wünsche, 113, 115, 124.